The BIG BOOK Of BUILDING, MODS & CIRCUITS

MINECRAFT®™

Imagine it ... Create it ... Build it

TRIUMPH
BOOKS

This book is available in quantity at special discounts for your group or organization.
For further information, contact:

Triumph Books LLC
814 North Franklin Street
Chicago, Illinois 60610
Phone: (312) 337-0747
www.triumphbooks.com

Printed in U.S.A.
ISBN: 978-1-62937-180-1

Content packaged by Mojo Media, Inc.
Joe Funk: Editor
Jason Hinman: Creative Director
Trevor Talley: Writer

Contents

Introduction 4

What's New And Upcoming In Minecraft 6

Biomes 8

Ores & Minerals 20

Friends & Foes 24

Navigation 40

Mining Better 48

Combat 60

Farming & Advanced Agriculture 68

What To Do When 76

Guide To Mini-Games & Online Play 86

Servers: Worlds Waiting For You Online 98

Software To Boost Your Builds 106

Minecraft On The Web 110

Skins, Resource Packs And Shaders 118

Redstone Basics 124

Master The Mods 146

10 Awesome Builds 168

The Future Of Minecraft 178

Heroes Of Minecraft 180

Minecraft, YouTube And A New
Kind Of Star 186

HERE'S YOUR PICKAXE & HELMET

Minecraft is truly on a roll. With every passing year, the game gets on new platforms, gets in the hands of new players and gets more and more massively popular. And there's a good reason for that.

Put simply, Minecraft is one of the most inventive, creative and unique games ever created. Posing as a simple survival and world-building game, Minecraft fans have taken its unique system and caused it to blossom into something much more: a global cultural phenomenon.

With so many people taking the plunge into the crazy, block-filled world of Minecraft, it's no wonder you might be curious about the game. But like many before you, you might be asking yourself, "What is it about this low-resolution existence that people like so much?"

What is Minecraft?

Let's get this out of the way right off the bat: Minecraft is not like other games.

The basic premise of Minecraft is that you are a character who has spawned into a world that's entirely made up of materials, which you can harvest, and populated by creatures called mobs, which you can kill. Your immediate goal is this: survive.

There are animals and plants for food, and materials to build a shelter, but the world of Minecraft is not all out to help you. At night, hostile, dangerous mobs come out to try their best to kill you and maybe even wreck your home a bit.

Once you've secured your defenses against the dark, dark night, however, the resemblance to a typical video game ends.

Minecraft has little plot, the graphics are basic (though we think they're cool looking) and it rarely tells you what to do next. So why is Minecraft so popular?

MORE THAN SURVIVING

It's simple: Minecraft is whatever you want it to be. That might sound like exaggeration, but it really isn't. Everything you see in the world of Minecraft can be changed, from knocking down a tall mountain, to drying up a lake to building enormous structures that tower into the sky anywhere you like.

This is possible because everything in the environment of Minecraft is created by blocks, each of which is made up of a resource such as Stone or Wood. These blocks can be removed by "breaking" them, and you can then either use them to build the world the way you'd like, or you can turn them into even more materials and items. All it takes is a little exploring, and you can find the resources to create just about anything.

EXPLORE, EXPLORE AND EXPLORE FURTHER

And Minecraft does not shirk or mess about when it comes to giving you plenty to explore. One of the masterstrokes of this modern classic game is that it uses complex algorithms to create massively diverse and unique worlds to explore every time you load it.

There are endless deserts populated by thriving villages and cut through with winding rivers. There are towering snowy mountains that cast shadows over sweeping plains dotted with flowers, lava fields and cave entrances. There are even multiple dimensions and an underground filled with ruins and adventures that will take you dozens of hours to fully explore, if you can survive the creatures that dwell there.

THE REAL REASON MINECRAFT IS GREAT

In the end though, there's one reason Minecraft has cemented its status as a truly great game, and that's this: Minecraft is only limited by your imagination.

If you can think of it, you can build it or make it happen. That is, if you know how the game works.

We want you to be the best Minecrafter you can be, and it's a time-honored Minecraft tradition for veteran players to pass down their knowledge to newcomers. Here you'll find everything you need to get started and begin your first monumental creation, but don't get us wrong, this guide isn't just for the noobs.

The Big Book is also full of advanced info, exclusive strategies and tips and tricks that even the best pros will find useful. With chapters that take you from the early stages of the game all the way through to advanced tactics for combat, mining, farming, exploration, Redstone and just about everything else in the game, this book is meant to be your go-to for any question or issue you might have about Minecraft.

LET'S BUILD

Now, with the goal of surviving the dark night in order to bring staggering creations of beauty and wonder into the digital world, pick up your phone, mouse or Xbox controller, crack open this book and start up a fresh world of Minecraft.

There's a world of infinite imagination and excitement waiting for you just on the other side of this page, so as we say here at the 'Crafter, grab your pickaxe and let's dig in!

It's time to build.

WHAT'S NEW AND UPCOMING IN MINECRAFT

When Microsoft bought Mojang, the creators and maintainers of Minecraft, back in September 2014 for 2.5 billion dollars, we knew it'd only be a matter of time before they started using their considerable power to implement some big changes into Minecraft, and some cool new things.

This chapter is all about looking to what we should see in the game coming up soon, as well as what has recently been released. These are exciting days for Minecraft indeed, and it seems like it's only beginning!

THE WINDOWS 10 EDITION

On July 29, 2015, the brand spankin' new version of Windows 10 was released, and with it Microsoft made the first steps toward creating a version of Minecraft that will play across all platforms, so that players on different devices can play in the same world! Windows 10 Edition is basically another version of Minecraft separate from the primary one. It's still a work in progress, and because it has to be able to run on all different platforms the same way, and that means that the Pocket Edition is the one that it is based on (so no super complex Redstone or anything yet), though it can be played on Xbox, Windows and Mac.

Things the Windows 10 Edition includes as of the writing of this book:

· SUPER fast creation and loading of worlds. Much faster than ever before, even on tablets!

· VERY far render distance. The render distance on vanilla Windows 10 Edition is faster and wayyyy farther than vanilla on the PC right now.

· Can use Xbox controllers to control.

· Multiplayer for up to 8 players over Xbox Live.

· New boat controls! Uses paddles instead of just moving about magically.

THE 1.9 UPDATE

The other HUGE news upcoming in the Minecraft world since the acquisition by Microsoft is the next update coming soon for the regular game. Of course, we don't know everything about this update yet, but enough has been released that we know a few things to expect. Here's a sampling of what's to come in the 1.9 update:

· Dual-wielding weapons and tools! Hold one in one hand, one in the other, and use both!

· Updates to The End. The End is getting a complete overhaul, including a better Dragon, a new mob named the Shulker, End Cities (big procedurally generated dungeon-type things), a tree-like plant called the Chorus Plant, Purpur material (made from Chorus Fruit, a new building material) and the End Ship (a boat floating in The End with treasures like a Brewing Stand in it).

· Spectral Arrows, which make players glow when hit. Will glow with the player's team color if on a multiplayer team.

· Beetroot, a new food.

· And more! We can't wait.

A pair of towers sits atop an Extreme Hills Biome.

BIOMES

What exactly do we mean by "Biomes"?

This might seem like an easy question to answer, and in a basic sense, the definition of "Biome" in Minecraft is pretty straightforward: Biomes are the different types of land you can find in Minecraft. However, there are actually two distinct types of Biomes that can be found in the game. For this book, we'll call them "Area Biomes" and "Feature Biomes," respectively, and you'll notice when you play that you'll often find them existing together, with the Feature Biome set within the larger Area Biome.

Area Biomes: We use this term to refer to the large sections of land that contain certain plants, mobs and aesthetics (for instance, Desert Biomes are mostly yellow and tan with little life, while the Jungle Biome is lush with life and is full of deep greens and browns). When running around the world of Minecraft, Area Biomes are what you'll most often be in when above ground, and the border between one Area Biome and the next is usually pretty easy to see, as the ground will change color from one Biome to the next. Think of Area Biomes as different types of nature, or environments.

Feature Biomes: Where Area Biomes refer to areas where certain plants and mobs live, Feature Biomes are more recognizable by their shape. Think of them as natural structures, including Beaches, Rivers, Ravines and Hills. Caves aren't technically considered a Biome, but we've included them with Feature Biomes as they have many similarities.

WHY YOU SHOULD KNOW YOUR BIOMES

Other than the obvious reason that you want to be an ultra-level, super-guru, Minecrafter genius-person, there is an important practical reason that knowing your various Biomes is a great idea: some items, mobs, structures and even Feature Biomes exist mostly or even exclusively in specific Biomes.

For instance, say you're looking for a lot of Wood and you need it really quickly. Well, if you know your Biomes, you know to stay away from the Desert Biome, and hopefully there's a Jungle Biome nearby. Ready to go cave-diving? The Extreme Hills Biome is your best bet, and you're unlikely to find what you're looking for in the Jungle.

The fact that not all Biomes are created equal, and that some contain resources you'll need more often (like Wood) and others don't, also makes it important to know Biomes at the beginning of your game when choosing a spot for a home. There's nothing worse than building a super-sweet house and then realizing that you'll have to hoof it about five minutes to the north to get more Wood because you built your home in a Biome without many trees.

THE BIOME BREAKDOWN

So now that you know why you'll be an even better Crafter when you get your Biome game on lock-down, let's get into it! While we're not going to get into the crazy math that goes behind each Biome (it's out there online, if you're interested), we are going to give you a basic idea of what each Biome is like, what you can find there, why you might want to visit it and whether or not it's a good spot to build a base. We've simplified the info for the Feature Biomes, as they are more about looks and things don't spawn exclusively in them.

PLAINS BIOME:

What It's Like: One of the more common Biomes, the Plains (or Grasslands) is full of Grass, Flowers and some smaller trees. It usually features plenty of mobs (both hostile and friendly) roaming about, and you can sometimes find caves, lakes, Villages and Lava pools scattered around it.

Unique Items, Resources and Mobs: None

Reasons to Visit: It's peaceful and has plentiful Grass (for Seeds) and peaceful mobs to hunt. It's also good for later in the game when you have a lot of resources and want a big space to build something in.

Good for a Base? Only on the edges. Building too far into the Plains will lead to lots of time spent running to Forest Biomes and others with more resources, but building on the edges of the Plains can be fun.

FOREST BIOME

What It's Like: Trees, trees and more Trees! Another very common Biome, the Forest Biome is one of the most useful early in the game, as they provide large amounts of Wood.

Unique Items, Resources and Mobs:

· Wolves are often found wandering outside of Forest Biomes, but they tend to spawn here.

· Though you can find plenty of trees elsewhere, the Jungle Biome is the only Biome with a greater concentration of trees (and those are almost exclusively Jungle Trees).

Reasons to Visit: You need Wood! Also, they are excellent for mob hunting, even in the day, as the shadows created by trees are ideal for keeping hostile mobs spawned.

Good for a Base? Absolutely! The easy access to Wood makes Forests great for your first base, though you might want to find an edge of the Forest so that you don't have to clear out so many leaves.

DESERT BIOME

What It's Like: Sparse of life and resources, the Desert is pretty cool-looking, but is not a great place to spend large amounts of time unless it is near another, more resource-heavy Biome.

Unique Items, Resources and Mobs:

· Cactus grows in the Desert and can be used for traps and decoration.

· Sand and Sandstone, while not exclusive to the Desert, will be found in the largest amounts here.

· Dry Bushes also grow here and are mostly used for decoration.

Reasons to Visit: The three primary reasons people head to the Desert are Sand, Cactus and Desert Villages. For whatever reason, Villagers love the Desert, and you'll often find a Village or two within. Primarily, however, Deserts are best for grabbing Sand for making Glass and Sandstone.

Good for a Base? Only at the edge of the Desert and another Biome. It's good to have a Desert near your base (as you'll probably want Glass at some point), but its utter lack of trees is a huge drawback for building a base there.

SWAMP BIOME

What It's Like: Lots of little bits of land surrounded by Water. Features short Oak Trees covered in Vines, and often has Mushrooms and Lily Pads around.

Unique Items, Resources and Mobs:
· Lily Pads are most commonly found here. These are fun decorations, but you can also build bridges across Water with them.

Reasons to Visit: Swamps are okay for Wood, but you're always better off finding a Forest Biome when you need large amounts. Most of the reason players go to Swamps is to find the resources that are common there, such as Lily Pads, Vines and Mushrooms.

Good for a Base? Can be a cool-looking spot for your home, but you'll need to have a Forest nearby in the long-run.

EXTREME HILLS BIOME

What It's Like: You'll know this one when you see it: huge hills with massive cliffs, overhangs and even waterfalls. One of the most interesting-looking Biomes there is, and a fan-favorite.

Unique Items, Resources and Mobs: None as of now (Emerald Ore is exclusive here but not yet included on the console versions of Minecraft).

Reasons to Visit: When looking for Caves and resources, this is by far your best bet. Extreme Hills Biomes are absolutely riddled with Cave openings, and because there's so much exposed rock, you'll often be able to simply look around outside for Coal and Iron Ore.

Good for a Base? Again, yes, but only if there's a Forest nearby. One trick is to start at a Forest, collecting a lot of Wood and Saplings, and then move to a nearby Extreme Hills Biome to build your home. As they're great for caves, it helps you later in the game, and you can always plant your Saplings on the Extreme Hills (which looks awesome too).

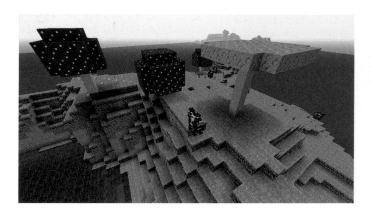

MUSHROOM ISLAND BIOME

What It's Like: Maybe the most unique Biome, this features purple-ish Mycelium as its primary building block and has Huge Mushrooms that look like trees. Always found out in the Ocean Biome.

Unique Items, Resources and Mobs:

· Mycelium, a unique Dirt-like building block that is purple/grey and which Mushrooms like to grow on.

· Mooshrooms hang out on the Mushroom Island. These are Cows that have Mushrooms growing on them. These are great food sources, as you can get Milk, Beef, Mushrooms and Mushroom Stew from them, as well as Leather.

· Giant Mushrooms are another great food source, as chopping them down gives you large amounts of Mushrooms.

Reasons to Visit: For one, there are no hostile mobs on these islands, so they're nice as sanctuaries. They're also very good for food, and if you can manage to get a Mooshroom back to your base, you'll have a constant plentiful food source.

Good for a Base? Nope. You could always build a secondary base on one, or a bridge or tunnel connecting your base to one, but because they are so isolated out in the Water, you're going to constantly have to go back to the main landmass to get other resources.

TAIGA BIOME

What It's Like: Can often be snowy and is a sort-of "Russian"-style forest with Spruce Trees and Wolves.

Unique Items, Resources and Mobs:

· Another great place to find Wolves (though again, they aren't unique to here).

· The best bet for Spruce Trees.

Reasons to Visit: Mostly just to chop down Spruce Trees or find Wolves to tame.

Good for a Base? Can be, though you'll be stuck with just one Wood type for the most part. Mostly good for raiding for Spruce Wood.

JUNGLE BIOME

What It's Like: BIIIIIG trees. Like, really, really big trees. And lots of them. Tons of foliage in general, and usually some hilly areas and lakes.

Unique Items, Resources and Mobs:

- Jungle Trees. These are absolutely the best Wood resource out there, and you'll love finding a Jungle just to get at these giant trees. They can be as big as four times wider than a normal Tree and many, many times taller. You'll often find them covered in Vines as well.

- Cocoa Pods are sometimes found on Jungle trees and are used in food crafting.

- Ocelots! One of the cutest and most useful mobs, the Ocelot is very hard to catch but when tamed they can be used as pets or as guards against Creepers (that's right, Creepers hate Cats and won't go near 'em!)

Reasons to Visit: Get on top of Jungle Tree and chop down all the Wood you'll ever need (well, for about a project or so at least). You'll also want Cats at some point to protect your stuff, so Ocelot taming is a good reason as well.

Good for a Base? Sure! With all that Wood around, why not try a tree-house? You'll probably need to visit others for certain resources, but the Jungle is a great Biome for building, if you can clear out a spot.

OCEAN BIOME

What It's Like: Lots and lots of Water, going off into the distance. There are also underwater Caves and Squids!

Unique Items, Resources and Mobs:

- Squids can sometimes find their ways into Rivers, but you're mostly gonna find these neat little guys (that drop Ink Sacs) in the Ocean.

Reasons to Visit: If you're feeling adventurous and want to try an underwater cave, or if you need a Squid. They can also be pretty good for taking a Boat around, as you can explore the coast.

Good for a Base? Not at all. The Ocean has zero Wood and is hard to build in, not to mention breathe. Of course, everyone wants to have an underwater base at some point, so if you've got the resources, it's a fun place for a secondary home later in the game.

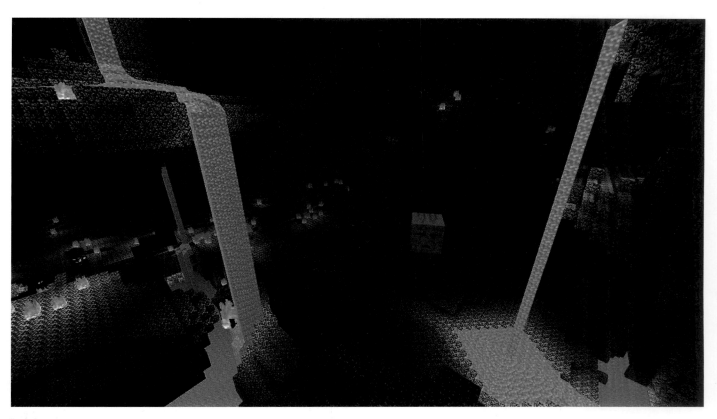

NETHER BIOME

What It's Like: Fire, Lava, things trying to kill you constantly, little in the way of food. Basically super, super hostile.

Unique Items, Resources and Mobs:
TONS. The Nether is like a whole new world, and most of what you'll find there is exclusive.

- Nether Rack is a red building block that when set on fire stays on fire.

- Nether Brick is made from Nether Rack and has a similar relationship to Stone's relationship to Cobblestone.

- Soul Sand is a building block that makes things move slow, great for docks for your Boat.

- Glowstone is a building block that produces light.

- Nether Wart is a plant resource that is used in recipes and only found in the Nether.

- Magma Cubes are like Slimes, but made of fire and Lava and are pretty darn dangerous.

- Ghasts are huge, flying creatures that shoot fireballs and will seriously mess you up.

- Zombie Pigmen are passive, unless you attack them, and they wield weapons.

- Blazes are some of the more dangerous mobs, floating around and shooting Fire Charges at you.

You'll need to kill some at some point if you want to make it to The End.

Reasons to Visit: Besides all of the unique resources, the mobs and the unique things they drop, you'll need to get to the Nether to get items you need to get to The End.

Good for a Base? You can try, but Beds explode on placement in the Nether, so don't expect to get too comfy. Take Stone and Cobblestone with you, as you're going to need something to protect you from Ghast blasts.

FEATURE BIOMES

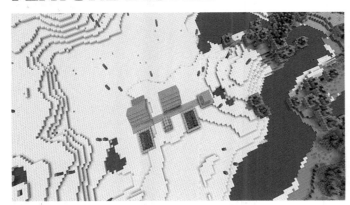

RIVER BIOME

What It's Like: Neat little rivers, cutting through the land and giving it definition.

Reasons to Visit: They look very cool, and it's always fun to build near one.

RAVINE BIOME

What It's Like: Giant gashes cut into the land that go down very, very far. These can be on the surface or underground, and can often contain waterfalls and Lava falls.

Reasons to Visit: They can be neat to build across or on either side of, but mostly they are just spectacular for getting ore and finding caves, as you can just look at the wall and see where the deposits are.

HILLS BIOME

What It's Like: Just plain ole hills, these can occur on many Biomes including Desert, Plains and Forests.

Reasons to Visit: Good for building on top of, as they offer a view of the surrounding mobs at night.

BEACH BIOME

What It's Like: Little bits of Sand on the edge of Water.

Reasons to Visit: Mostly just for Sand, and sometimes they have Clay as well!

FEATURE BIOMES

CAVE BIOME

What It's Like: Winding, often-complex tunnels through the ground, full of hostile mobs.

Reasons to Visit: These are your best-bet for running into the best resources and structures in the game (like Diamond, Redstone, Fortresses and Abandoned Mineshafts). You'll be spending a lot of time in caves, and it's a good idea to find one very big one and build a little base in it to explore from.

"SNOWY" BIOMES

What It's Like: Many Biomes have "cold" or "Snowy" versions where you can find Ice and Snow, as well as get actual snow-falling animations. Plains, Taiga, Rivers and Beaches can all have "Snowy" versions.

Reasons to Visit: You can get Snowballs here, which can be turned into Snow Blocks. Ice is also fun to use, as you slip across it, and the "Snowy" Biomes just look plain awesome.

DEEP OCEAN BIOME

What It's Like: The Ocean Biome, except with massive underwater mountains and Ravines.

Reasons to Visit: Same as the Ocean Biome, but good for giant underwater structures.

A Jungle Biome sits just above a Cave Biome giving this area a quite cool look.

"Infinite power just isn't very interesting, no matter what game you're playing. It's much more fun when you have a limited tool set to use against the odds. Usually, a new player to Minecraft doesn't make it through the first night. They're just not prepared for the danger. It's a harsh lesson but it establishes the rules."

— Notch on why Minecraft is the way it is

MESA BIOME

What It's Like: Dry and covered in beautiful bands of Clay and Sand of different types. These are pretty hard to find, but there's no better source of Clay in the game. There are two types of Mesas: the regular Mesa and the Bryce Mesa, which features tall spires of Clay as well as the regular hills and mesas.

Unique Items, Resources and Mobs:
The Mesa Biome has
· Hardened Clay
· 6 varieties of Stained Clay
· Red Sand and Red Sandstone

Reasons to Visit:
The Clay, and because they look great!

Good for a Base? Only if it's near a Forest. There's no wood on the Mesa Biome.

SAVANNA BIOME

What It's Like: Somewhat like a Plain Biome with a few more short rises and falls, but with dry Grass and Acacia Trees. Like Plains, the Savanna can spawn Horses, and like a Desert, there's no rain on the Savanna.

Unique Items, Resources and Mobs:
· Acacia Trees
· Horses

Reasons to Visit:
That cool, colorful Acacia Wood, and Horses.

Good for a Base? If there's a Forest nearby, then yeah, they can make for very picturesque base locations.

Ice Plain Spikes

BIOME VARIATIONS

Many Biomes have variations on the basic Biome, including the Mega Taiga and a variety of "M-type" Biomes. Here are the different variations and what makes them different:

Ice Plains Spikes: Plains with snow and a large number of spike structures made of Ice blocks sticking into the air. Some are very tall, going up over 50 blocks

Cold Taiga M: Mountainous variation on the Taiga

Extreme Hills M: Higher peaks, mostly made of Gravel, not many trees

Taiga M: Mountains on the non-snowy version of the Taiga

Mega Taiga: Has giant Spruce Trees, has Podzol blocks and Moss Stone boulders

Extreme Hills+/+ M: Adds Spruce and Oak Trees, the M version has fewer of these but massive Gravel mountains

Stone Beach: Where the Water runs into Stone and not Sand

Plains M: Plains with Water patches and a little bit of mountains

Sunflower Plains: Large patches of lovely Sunflowers on the Plains

Flower Forest: Just like it sounds: beautiful flowers of all kinds on the floor of a regular Forest

Swampland M: More hills than on the Swamps, no Witch Huts

Jungle M: More mountains and heavy plant-life

Jungle Edge/M: A more sparse version of the Jungle without the big trees that happens at the edge of Jungle Biomes. M version is more mountain-y

Birch Forest M: Tall Birch Trees

Birch Forest Hills/M: Adds hills to the Birch Forest, M version adds mountains and tall Birch Trees

Roofed Forest/M: A very cool Biome where Dark Oak Trees grow so close together that it's actually dark beneath their leaves. Contains Huge Mushrooms and other mushrooms, and hostile mobs can survive the day there. M version has cliffs on the edges

Desert M: Patches of water can be found here, unlike the regular Desert

Savanna M: Crazy, weird mountains mixed into the Savanna. Can create the largest natural mountains outside of using the AMPLIFIED setting

Plateau/Plateau M: Hills Biome with flattened tops, often found in Savanna and Mesas. M version for Savanna is much taller and steeper, while for Mesa it's flatter

ORES & MINERALS

ORES/MINERALS

When we're talking about the "mining" part of Minecraft, these are the things you'll be looking to find, for the most part. All ores and minerals form in "veins," or pockets that are usually surrounded by Stone, Dirt and Gravel (though sometimes Water and Lava too). They are much harder to find than most blocks, and they are used in most of the complex or advanced creations.

Note: You can craft solid blocks of each of the ores and minerals for use in decoration or certain recipes.

COAL

Types: Charcoal, Coal
Found: Charcoal—Burn
Wood in a Furnace, Coal—the Overworld in formations at any level (1% of Stone blocks are Coal)
Used In: Torches, smelting, Fire Charge, running Powered Minecarts
Drops: 2/3 chance of experience dropping
Best Tool to Use: Pickaxe

The most plentiful ore is Coal, and that's good because you're going to need a whole lot of it. Coal is what makes Torches, which are the primary light source in your game. Without Coal, you won't have any Torches, and you probably won't be able to see. Luckily, you can either burn Wood in Furnaces to make Charcoal or find Coal deposits easily in formations. Both work the same, despite their different names. Coal is also one of the best fuels for smelting in Furnaces (behind Lava Buckets and Blaze Rods). Covet your Coal, kids.

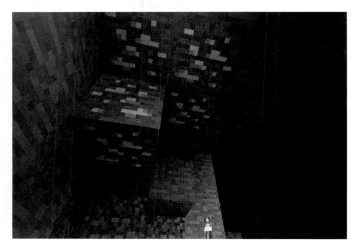

IRON

Found: Overworld from layer 1-63
Used In: Iron tools and armor, Buckets, Minecarts, Cauldron, Rails, Flint and Steel, Compass, Piston, Iron Door, and Iron Bars
Best Tool to Use: Stone Pickaxe or better required
If Diamond is the most coveted ore, Iron is the second, because Iron is necessary for so many important items. Whether building a railway with Minecarts, moving Water orLlava, setting a Nether Portal alight, trying to make a Map or even just mine Diamond and other rare materials, you'll need Iron. Iron is pretty common, luckily, though not nearly so as Coal. Look for it underground below sea level.

GOLD

Found: Overworld from layer 1-32
Used In: Gold Ingot, which makes Gold tools and Armor, Golden Apples, Clocks and Powered Rails
Best Tool to Use: Iron Pickaxe or better required
Gold is a very rare ore, with only 0.1473% of the underground of the world having Gold Ore in it. It can be crafted into Gold Ingots, whose main use is to craft Clocks, Golden Apples and Powered Rails. Gold items like tools and armor are weak, but can be enchanted, though the benefits rarely outweigh the cost. Gold tools are however the fastest mining tools in the game, but they also break the easiest (even easier than Wood tools).

NETHER QUARTZ ORE

Found: The Nether
Used In: Drops Nether Quartz Crystal, used in Comparators and Daylight Sensors (not yet in console) and Nether Quartz Blocks
Best Tool to Use: Wooden Pickaxe or better required
There's only one ore found in the Nether, and that's Nether Quartz. This is about as common as Iron and found on all layers of the Nether, but as of right now, the items that its drop (Nether Quartz Crystal) is used for are not yet implemented in the console version of the game. This should change soon.

DIAMOND

Found: Overworld from layer 1-16
Used In: Diamond tools and armor, Jukebox, Enchantment Table
Best Tool to Use: Iron Pickaxe or better required
Diamond is king. No seriously, in Minecraft, you want Diamond, more Diamond and all the Diamond. This is because Diamond makes the second fastest and longest lasting tools in the game at mining and harvesting, it can mine any other block, it makes the best weapons and armor and it's necessary for some recipes. Unfortunately, Diamond is also the hardest material to find, behind Emerald. Diamond is only in small deposits in the bottom 16 layers of the game, and it's only mineable with an Iron or Diamond Pickaxe. To find Diamond, you'll need to look in those low levels and try to find Lava, which it's often nearby. A note: you need Diamond tools to mine Obsidian, which you need to get to the Nether, which you probably need to do to get to The End.

REDSTONE

Found: Overworld from layer 1-16
Used In: Redstone mechanisms and circuits, Compass, Clock, Note Block
Best Tool to Use: Iron Pickaxe or better required
Another mineral found deep, deep down, Redstone is much more common than Diamond, and in fact will drop multiple pieces of Redstone for each block. It's one of the most interesting materials in the game due to it being the thing you need to create powered circuits and mechanisms. Redstone placed by itself acts like a wire connecting mechanisms to each other and power (which comes from Redstone Torches, Buttons, Levers or Pressure Plates), and when used with those mechanisms and other Redstone items, you can create complex machinery and devices. Look for Redstone by Lava.

LAPIS LAZULI

Found: Overworld from layer 1-32
Used In: Dying things blue
Best Tool to Use: Stone Pickaxe or better required

Lapis Lazuli is fairly rare in the game, but it also drops multiple pieces when it breaks, and it's not used for anything except to dye Wool blue. It's fun to come across, especially if you love blue, but it isn't as valuable as some of the other ores.

EMERALD ORE

Found: Overworld only in Extreme Hills Biomes between layers 4-32
Used In: Drops Emeralds, used to trade with Villagers
Best Tool to Use: Iron Pickaxe or better required

By far the rarest mineral in Minecraft, the Emerald Ore block is only found in the Extreme Hills Biome and there are usually somewhere between 3-8 blocks of it per chunk in such Biomes. When mined, it drops 1 Emerald, which is used to trade with Villagers to procure items. Emeralds are highly prized by players, as the items that can be procured with them tend to be very valuable.

FRIENDS & FOES

It only takes a few seconds in Survival Mode to realize that your character in Minecraft is not alone. Nope, the world of Minecraft is a full one, teeming with everything from tiny Chickens to Wolves to Zombie Pigmen to the giant Ghast, and if you're going to thrive in this crowded land, you're gonna need to know a bit about these creatures, known as "mobs."

Notes:

1. This section focuses on location, behavior, drops and combat. For breeding, see the Mining & Farming section.

2. The Attack stats are approximate. Attack can change somewhat depending on circumstances and exact numbers have yet to be confirmed for the Xbox 360 console version of the game.

3. Health, Armor and Attack are measured in half-icons, so 1 "heart" icon = 2 Health, one "sword" icon = 2 Attack, and one "chestplate" icon = 2 Armor.

PEACEFUL MOBS

There are quite a few mobs out there that won't ever attack you, no matter how many times you punch them in the face or otherwise pester them. These mobs are considered "peaceful."

SHEEP

Sheep are everywhere, they are not smart and you will need them for Beds. Sheep tend to spawn in flocks and then roam about, and since they can both jump 1 block high and swim, they end up all over the place.

Sheep are usually white (81.836% chance) but can also spawn as dark grey, light grey, or black (5%), brown (3%) or pink (0.164%), and whatever color they are is the color of Wool you will get from them. Wool can be gathered either by killing the Sheep or by using Shears on it (1 block for killing, 1-3 for shearing). You can also dye sheep to change the color of their Wool.

IRON GOLEM

The mighty Iron Golem! These tough dudes spawn naturally in Villages with 10 Villagers and 21 houses or more, and they serve to protect the Village from Zombie sieges. Additionally, players can craft them with 4 Blocks of Iron in a T formation with a Pumpkin stuck on top as the head. They are very powerful, but they will only protect Villagers, not the player, and they will wander away from the player if there is nothing keeping them from doing so (a barrier).

MOOSHROOM

A rarer version of the Cow, the Mooshroom is a Cow that's been infected by Mushrooms. You can only find these guys in the uncommon Mushroom Biome, but they're even better than Cows for food and materials.

This is because, in addition to what a Cow drops, you can also get infinite Mushroom Stew (3 food units, 7.2 hunger saturation). On top of that, if you ever really need Mushrooms, you can use Shears on the Mooshroom and get 5.

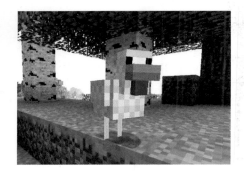

CHICKEN

Chickens may be small and easy to kill, but they also drop a ton of useful items and are easy to farm. You usually find Chickens spread out across the ground and Water,

and they can fall without taking damage, so they can end up in deep pits and ravines.

Chickens drop three potential food items: Eggs (used in cooking), Raw Chicken (2 units of the food bar, 1.2 hunger saturation [see Farming & Mining for more info], 30% chance of food poisoning) or Cooked Chicken (3 food units, 7.2 hunger saturation) if it was killed by fire. Chickens also drop Feathers, which are used in crafting Arrows.

COW

Another pack wanderer, Cows often spawn in groups of 4-10 then wander off, sometimes even falling down cliffs and killing themselves.

Cows are one of the best sources of food, as Raw Beef gives 3 food units and 1.8 hunger saturation (no risk of poison), Steak gives 4 food units and 12.8 hunger saturation and Milk is used to cure status effects like poison and in cooking Cakes. Steak is the most balanced food item in the game, and Milk is infinite, making Cows

very good to farm. Their other drop, Leather, is used in crafting the lowest level of armor.

OCELOT/CAT

Released when the Jungle Biome was added to the various versions of the game, the Ocelot/Cat is the cat lover's answer to the Wolf/Dog, and it's both super cute and super useful. Though they do not attack or cause damage at all, when tamed with an uncooked Fish, the Ocelot turns into a Cat. The Cat can either follow the character or be told to sit, and it will scare Creepers away from whatever area it's in! This makes Cats insanely useful at a base or important parts of your map. To tame, simply hold out an un-cooked Fish and wait 'til an Ocelot approaches. Feed the Fish to the Ocelot, and there's a 1/3 chance it'll turn into a Cat. Both Cats and Ocelots can breed by putting them into love mode with Fish.

PIG

Pigs spawn just about everywhere that's not underground, and their initial group is 3-4 Pigs, so you can often find quite a few together. Pig meat comes as Raw or Cooked Porkchops, and it gives identical health benefits to Raw Beef and Steak, respectively (3 food units, 1.8 hunger saturation / 4 food units, 12.8 hunger saturation), making Pigs a good source of food. It is possible to find a Saddle in a Chest, put it on the Pig and ride it around. To control the movement of the Pig, you need a Carrot on a Stick equipped.

WOLF

Though they start out neutral and will become hostile if attacked (and will attack in groups), Wolves can be "tamed" by feeding them Bones. You'll know a Wolf is successfully tamed when it gets a collar around its neck and starts following you.

Tamed wolves follow the player and attack any mobs that attack the player or are attacked by the player except Creepers. They are most effective versus Zombies and Skeletons, less against Spiders, Cave Spiders and Endermen and almost not at all against Creepers, Magma Cubes and Slimes. You can tell the health of a Wolf by the angle that its tail is pointing. A tail that is all the way up means full health, and all the way down means very low health, with corresponding positions in-between. To raise the health of your Wolf, feed it any meat, including Rotten Flesh (which won't hurt it). Wolves also have special behavioral traits when it comes to mobility. A Wolf told to follow you that gets outside of a 20x20x10 block from the player will automatically teleport to the player, unless there's no room for it to do so. Additionally, you can tell a wolf to "sit" with Left Trigger, which makes it stay where it is until otherwise ordered.

BATS

Bats are another mob that doesn't hurt the player at any point and will spawn anywhere where there is a light level of 3 or less below layer 63 in the world. They don't drop anything at all (not even experience), but they are pretty cool because they'll hang upside down to sleep on solid blocks, and then flap away when players approach like real bats. They're more for atmosphere than anything, and between October 20 and November 4 (so around Halloween), they'll spawn in a light level or 7 or less anywhere. Fun, spooky times in Minecraft!

SQUID

The only Water mob out there, the Squid will not attack and just drops Ink Sacs. They do make cool pets if you can trap them, though.

SNOW GOLEM

Snow Golems are creatures that are crafted by stacking two Snow Blocks on top of each other (4 Snowballs = 1 Snow Block) and topping it off with a Pumpkin.

Snow Golems are very weak and do no damage to any creature except Blazes and the Ender Dragon, and they are damaged by the Nether, Deserts, Jungles and Water of any kind. However, they do throw Snowballs at most hostile mobs (not Creepers, however), which pushes the mob back slightly and keeps them away when used in groups.

VILLAGER

Villagers hang out in, not surprisingly, Villages, and they can breed with each other and trade with the player. Each Villager has a profession (Farmer, Librarian, Priest, Blacksmith, Butcher), and you can trade with them for profession-related items. Typically, Villagers request Emeralds for the items they offer for trade.

ZOMBIE PIGMAN

All over the Nether, you'll find Zombie Pigmen, usually in groups. They spawn in fours, but can gather together in larger groups, and they hang out in most parts of the Nether.

Like Villagers, this mob is humanoid and initially neutral to the player, but unlike Villagers, Zombie Pigmen most definitely will attack you if you hurt one. In fact, attacking a Pigman alerts any other Pigmen within a 32 block radius, who will all go hostile and come at the player with Swords.

RABBITS

The hippity-hoppity, ear floppity Rabbit is a newer peaceful mob that spawns in Forest Biomes of all types (including Jungle), Taiga, Savanna, Plains, Swamp and Extreme Hills Biomes. They will not attack you, and you can get Raw Rabbit from them, as well as Rabbit's Foot, a brewing ingredient that is a rare drop. Rabbits are usually in small packs of three, will eat wild Carrots and can be led and bred with Carrots (also bred with Dandelions), and Wolves will hunt them down and kill them. There are six different fur types for Rabbits, and you can also get a special-colored Rabbit by using a Name Tag to name the Rabbit "Toast," which is a memorial to a player's missing rabbit in real life. There is a hostile version of the Rabbit called the Killer Bunny that is white with red eyes and will attack players and Wolves, but it does not spawn naturally and must be put in the world with commands.

HOSTILE MOBS

Now, these are the guys in Minecraft who want nothing more than to bite you, poison you, shoot you full of arrows, light you on fire, punch you in the face, blow you up and otherwise attempt to make you no more. Even with the best gear, a few of these guys ganging up on you can mean a quick death, often far from home, especially if you don't know their tendencies and weaknesses. Get familiar with these guys as much as possible, and it most definitely will save your life.

CREEPER

Ah, the Creeper. He's the unofficial mascot of the game, the sneakiest mob and the one you'll find yourself most dreading.

When Creepers get within two blocks of you (so one separating), their "countdown" starts, and you have 1.5 seconds before it blows up all of the blocks in about a 6x6x6 area around it. Yep, it's a pain. The only warning you get for this is a slight "hiss" sound when it gets close, and since they will attack any players they see within 16 blocks and are good at finding paths to you, it's pretty likely that you'll have at least one Creeper death in your Minecraft experience. This is made even more likely by the fact that they can survive in daylight, unlike most hostile mobs.

The good news is that Creepers can't blow up when they see you through Glass or a Door, and if you kill them from a distance or before they can do their countdown, they will die without exploding and will even drop Gunpowder, which you can use to make TNT.

A harder drop to get from a Creeper is a Music Disc, which requires the Creeper be killed by a Skeleton's Arrow. Because of their ability to blow up your hard work, it's best to protect yourself from Creepers by paying attention to your surroundings and building safely where they can't get to you. Because, as they say, that'ssssss a very nice house you've got there...It'd be a sssssshame if anything were to happen to it.

SPIDER

You're gonna see a lot of Spiders. Spiders are neutral until they've been exposed to darkness or attacked. This means that a Spider found in daylight will be neutral, but if he happens to wander into a dark area, he's gonna go hostile and stay that way. Spiders that start off in dark areas and move to light will remain hostile, however.

Despite their small attack, Spiders are dangerous because they can climb walls as if all blocks had Ladders on them and they can jump up to 3 blocks high. They also can see players through walls, meaning that if there's a hostile Spider within 16 blocks of you, it knows you're there and is trying to get to you, and they can even fit through one block high spaces.

To be safe around Spiders, wear armor, carry weapons and make sure your shelter is enclosed and well-lit. If you do kill a Spider, it may drop the very useful String or Spider Eyes.

SPIDER JOCKEY

A very rare mob, these have a 1% chance of spawning anytime a Spider does. They include a Skeleton archer riding on top of a Spider, both of which otherwise behave normally and take damage individually. Because of this, Spider Jockeys spawn, move and see like Spiders, though the Skeleton will simply attack anytime it sees you, whether the Spider is hostile or not. On top of that, the Skeleton can suffocate or burn in daylight, leaving the Spider on its own.

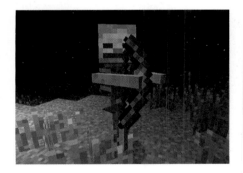

SKELETON

Skeletons are major pests in Minecraft because they spawn just about everywhere there's darkness and they attack with arrows from a distance. If you're being attacked in a dark cave and you can't see where it's coming from, then you've probably found a Skeleton.

Skeleton attacks don't do huge damage, however, and can even be entirely prevented by armor. You will want to make sure your shelter is completely sealed, however, because they can shoot through gaps. Skeletons also burn up in daylight.

Skeletons have two very useful drops when killed: Bones and Arrows. Bones can be turned into Bonemeal for use in farming, and picking up Arrows from Skeletons is a lot easier than crafting them.

ZOMBIE

Another of the most common mobs, Zombies wander around the Overworld at night looking for you and your fleshy friends so they can feed on you. Zombies also attack Villages in swarms called Zombie Sieges and can eventually break down doors, both in Villages and otherwise.

Zombies attack by touching you, and they can quickly take your health down if they trap you in a small area. The main reason for killing Zombies, other than survival, is that they drop Rotten Flesh. This stuff can be eaten by your character in an emergency (4 food units, 80% chance of poisoning), but its main use is to feed tame Wolves. Like many mobs, Zombies burn during daylight.

ENDERMAN

From the deep, dark lands of The End, the Endermen come to the Overworld to shift blocks around, look awesome and punch you for looking at them. No joke. Endermen are special mobs that aren't hostile to start, but if you're within 64 blocks and your crosshair points at an Enderman above their legs, they will come at you.

Endermen have a pretty tough attack, which is made worse by their ability to teleport around. This also means they can show up almost anywhere, though they tend to avoid sunlight, rain and Water. Sunlight, rain, Water and fire make them neutral, and any contact with Water damages an Enderman—useful tips for combat. It's suggested to attack the legs as well, as the Enderman can't teleport when taking leg damage.

Fighting an Enderman can be necessary when attempting to go to The End, because finding the necessary Ender Pearls otherwise can be very difficult.

CAVE SPIDER

You won't run into Cave Spiders very often, as they only spawn in Abandoned Mineshafts from Monster Spawners, but they're much tougher than regular Spiders. To deal with Cave Spiders, you'll have to fight your way to their spawner and either break it or disable it.

Doing that is more than likely going to mean a bite or two from a Cave Spider, and since they're poisonous, you'll want to bring some Milk to counteract the effects.

SILVERFISH

Silverfish hang out in fake blocks called Monster Eggs in Strongholds and in caves in the Extreme Hills Biome. The Silverfish can make a Monster Egg out of a Cobblestone, Stone or Stone Brick block, and you can tell it's a Monster Egg by it taking longer than normal to break with a tool or quicker without one.

Breaking a Monster Egg releases a hostile Silverfish, and if it is attacked and not killed, it will wake every Silverfish in a 21x11x21 block radius and make them attack as well. Silverfish do damage every time you make a change on the Y axis (vertical) in relation to the Silverfish. You also hop every time you're damaged, which is a change on the Y axis, so Silverfish can do damage quickly.

SLIME

Only spawning below level 40, Slimes have three sizes. When the Slime is killed, it splits into 2-4 more Slimes of the next smallest size until it is made tiny and killed again.

Slimes are great for experience and are further useful for their drop, Slimeballs, which are used to make Sticky Pistons and Magma Cream. They are also one of the few hostile mobs that can survive sunlight.

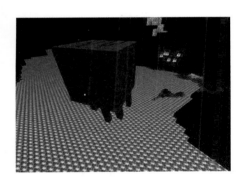

GHAST

The scourges of the Nether, Ghasts are huge and shoot at you with explosive fireballs from up to 100 blocks away. These fireballs do 17 damage at close range (8.5 hearts), but they also light the area around on fire, which deals more damage.

To defeat Ghasts, you'll need to build shelters that protect you from their line of site, and hit the Ghast fireballs away with your hand or item. Ghasts drop Gunpowder like Creepers as well as Ghast Tears, a potion ingredient.

MAGMA CUBE

Similar to Slimes, Magma Cubes are hopping creatures found in the Nether that also split into smaller Magma Cubes. The main differences, besides their appearance, is that they can survive falls, Lava and Water, jump 4 blocks high and do more damage than a Slime.

As with Slime, Magma Cubes are great for experience, and they also drop Magma Cream, another potion ingredient.

BLAZE

If you're looking for Blaze Powder, you'll need to find a Blaze, and these tough mobs only show up in Nether Forts. There, Blazes will start popping out once you're within 16 blocks of a Blaze Spawner and can spawn 1-4 at a time, meaning they will build in numbers quickly.

The best method for defeating Blazes is to kill those spawned by using weapons and Snowballs (which do 3 damage to the Blaze). While doing so, destroy or disable the Monster Spawner to avoid more. Snow Golems are also good against Blazes, but will melt in the Nether.

Blazes carry two rare items: Blaze Rods (used in creating Brewing Stands and Blaze Powder) and Glowstone Dust (used in brewing and making Glowstone). Since Blaze Powder is necessary to make an Eye of Ender (among other things), which you need to get to The End, many players find themselves needing to hunt Blazes at some point.

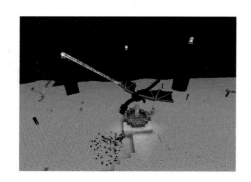

ENDER DRAGON

There's no greater foe in Minecraft than the Ender Dragon, and there are few greater challenges. Located in The End, the Ender Dragon has 200 health points and does huge damage in the Xbox 360 console version (the PC version has different attacks).

The Ender Dragon also gains health by having it beamed from a circle of Obsidian pillars that have Ender Crystals on the top. These will need to be destroyed before you can kill the Ender Dragon, either by shooting them with Arrows or (in the case of the caged Crystals) building to them and breaking them.

It's recommended to take enchanted Diamond weapons and armor and a lot of Obsidian to build with (it won't blow up like most blocks) to defeat the mighty Ender Dragon. Once you do, you'll be rewarded with 12,000 experience (enough to get you to level 78) and the infamous End Poem.

ENDERMITES

There are no hostile mobs smaller than the Endermite, and these little guys will comes at any player within 16 blocks of them. They will get hurt on Soul Sand and Endermen don't like them and will try to kill them if a player isn't close. They spawn very rarely: only when an Enderman teleports (a 15% chance) or when the player throws an Ender Pearl (5% chance). They only do two hearts of damage, but that can add up!

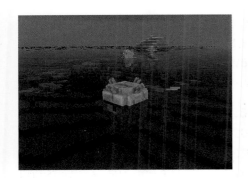

GUARDIAN/ELDER GUARDIAN

The Guardian and its big sibling the Elder Guardian are two dangerous Water-based mobs that only spawn in and around Ocean Monuments. They will attack automatically when they see a player, but will stop attacking if you go out of their line of sight. They have two attacks: firing a laser that does high damage, and shooting out spikes when a player gets close as a defense, which does less. The Elder Guardian only spawns three times in each Monument and also causes the player to move slower and break blocks slower by putting a "mining fatigue" status on any player within 50 blocks (once a minute), while the regular Guardians can spawn in much larger numbers and don't have the status effect ability.

WITHER SKELETON

A much badder, meaner version of the Skeleton that only spawns in Nether Fortresses in spots where the light level is 7 or lower. They move very fast as soon as they see a player, and they'll smack you not only with their Stone Sword, but also hit you with the Wither I effect, which will take your health bar down gradually. Weirdly, they can actually pick up Swords and armor dropped on the ground and use them. Very tough to kill, these guys!

WITHER

Besides the Ender Dragon, the only other boss mob in the game is the Wither, and boy is this three-headed meany a hard thing to fight. To find one, you actually have to make it similar to a Golem. Take Soul Sand and make an upright T shape two blocks tall and three wide, and put a Wither Skeleton Skull (drops sometimes when killing Wither Skeletons) on each Soul Sand block on the top of the T. The Wither will spawn and start moving around while its health bar grows (it's invulnerable at this stage), and then it will cause a very large explosion that will damage players and blocks, but not the Wither. When this happens, you can attack. The Wither is immune to fire, Lava, drowning and suffocation, and it will attack anything except other undead mobs. Its attack features shooting a "Wither skull" shot at anything in its area from each of its three heads, all of which can attack a different thing at once. It can fly, but at half health it will only go as high as its target, but it also gains invulnerability to Arrows with "Wither armor." Healing potions will hurt it, but other effects don't work, and it also will heal itself a half heart every 1-second. Its skulls will put the Wither II effect on anything hit, which drains health over time, and it will heal the Wither 5 health.

WIITCH

The Witch is a solitary mob that you don't see too often, but when you do, it's gonna be a scary time. Witches use splash Potions to do damage to players and to buff themselves against attack, making them potentially one of the most dangerous mobs in Minecraft. Witches can spawn anywhere in the Overworld with a light level of 7 of less, but they also automatically spawn in Witch huts, which are small houses in Swamp Biomes. If lightning hits close to a Villager, this will also turn the Villager into a Witch. Witches have a lot of items they can drop, as well as quite a few attacks (see chart).

PEACEFUL MOBS

Friend/Foe	Found	Health	Exp.	Drop	Follows (when in hand)
SHEEP	Overworld	8 (4 Hearts)	1-3	Wool (1, 1-3 if dropped) Raw Mutton (1-2)	Wheat
CHICKEN	Overworld	4 (2 Hearts)	1-3	Feathers (0-2) Raw Chicken (1) Cooked Chicken (1 if killed by fire) Egg (1 every 5-10 minutes if alive)	Any seed
COW	Overworld	10 (5 Hearts)	1-3	Leather (0-2) Raw Beef (1-3) Steak (1-3 if killed by fire) Milk (when Bucket is used on it)	Wheat
MOOSHROOM	Overworld (Mushroom Biome)	10 (5 Hearts)	1-3	Leather (0-2) Raw Beef (1-3) Steak (1-3 if killed by fire) Milk (when Bucket is used on it) Mushroom Stew (when Bowl is used on it) Red Mushroom (5 when sheared)	Wheat
PIG	Overworld	10 (5 Hearts)	1-3	Raw Porkchop (1-3) Cooked Porkchop (1-3 if killed by fire)	Wheat

Friend/Foe	Found	Health	Attack	Exp.	Drop	Follows (when in hand)
WOLF	Overworld (spawns on grass)	Wild: 8 (4 Hearts) Tamed: 20 (10)	Wild: 2 (1 Heart) Tamed: 4	1-3	None	Bone

Friend/Foe	Found	Health	Exp.	Drop
SQUID	Overworld (Water, spawns between levels 46-62)	10 (5 Hearts)	1-3	Ink Sac (1-3)
VILLAGER	Overworld (Villages)	20 (10 Hearts)	0	Nothing

Friend/Foe	Found	Health	Armor	Attack	Exp.	Drop
ZOMBIE PIGMAN	The Nether, rarely in the Overworld	20 (10 Hearts)	2	Easy: 5 Normal: 9 Hard: 13	5	Rotten Flesh (0-1)

PEACEFUL MOBS

Friend/Foe	Found	Health	Attack	Exp.	Drop
SNOW GOLEM	Created	4 (2 Hearts)	0 (only pushes most mobs) 3 (Blazes only) 1 (Ender Dragon)	0	Snowball (0-15)
OCELOT	Jungle	10 (5 hearts)	None (scares Creepers, however)	1-3	None
IRON GOLEM	Villages or Crafted by Player	100 (50 hearts)	7-21 (3.5-10.5 hearts)	0	Iron Ingot (3-5) Poppy (0-2)

Friend/Foe	Found	Health	Exp.	Drop	Follows (when in hand)
RABBIT	Overworld (many biomes)	10 (5 hearts)	1-3	Rabbit Hide (0-1)	Wheat
BAT	Overworld (in light level 3 or below, below level 63)	6 (3 hearts)	0	None	None

HOSTILE MOBS

Friend/Foe	Found	Spawns	Health	Attack	Exp.	Drop
CREEPER	Overworld or Nether	Light Level: 7 or less	20 (10 Hearts)	Depends on how close, Maximum: 49 (24.5 hearts)	5	Gunpowder (0-2 when killed but not exploded) Music Disc (when killed by an arrow from a Skeleton)
SPIDER	Overworld	Light Level: 7 or Less, But Can Survive in Light (goes Peaceful)	16 (8 Hearts)	Easy: 2 Normal: 2 Hard: 3	5	String (0-2) Spider Eye (0-1
SPIDER JOCKEY	Overworld	Light Level: 7 or Less, But Can Survive in Light (goes Peaceful)	Spider: 16 (8 Hearts) Skeleton: 20 (10)	Spider- Easy: 2 Normal: 2 Hard: 3 Skeleton- Easy: 2	5 for each	Spider: String (0-2) Spider Eye (0-1) Skeleton: Bone (0-2) Arrow (0-2)
SKELETON	Overworld or Nether	Light Level: 7 or less	20 (10 Hearts)	Easy: 2 Normal:3-4 Hard: 4-6	5	Arrow (0-2) Bone (0-2)

Friend/Foe	Found	Spawns	Armor	Health	Attack	Exp.	Drop
ZOMBIE	Overworld or Nether	Light Level: 7 or Less	2	20 (10 Hearts)	3-6 depending on health	5	Rotten Flesh Rare: Carrot, Iron Ingot, Potato

HOSTILE MOBS

Friend/Foe	Found	Spawns	Health	Attack	Exp.	Drop
ENDERMAN	Overworld or The End	Light Level: 7 or Less	40 (20 Hearts)	Easy: 4 Normal: 7 Hard: 10	5	Ender Pearl (0-1)
CAVE SPIDER	Overworld (Abandoned Mineshafts)	From Monster Spawner in Mineshaft Only	12 (6 Hearts)	Easy: 2 Normal: 2 (Poisoned) Hard: 3 (Poisoned) Poison Damage: 1 Every 1.5 seconds Normal: 7 Seconds Hard: 15 Seconds	5	String (0-2) Spider Eye (0-1)

Friend/Foe	Found	Spawns	Health	Attack	Exp.	Drop
SILVERFISH	Overworld (Strongholds and Rarely Underground in Extreme Hills Biomes)	From Monster Spawner (Strongholds) or Monster Egg (Fake Blocks, Strongholds and Extreme Hills Biomes)	8 (4 Hearts)	1	5	None
SLIME	Overworld	Below Level 40	Big: 16 (8 Hearts) Small: 4 (2) Tiny: 1 (0)	Big: 4 Small: 2 Tiny: 0	Big: 4 Small: 2 Tiny: 1	Slimeball (0-2, only from Tiny Slime)
GHAST	The Nether	Anywhere with space except in Nether Fortresses	10 (5 Hearts)	More the closer it gets, Max of 17	5	Gunpowder (0-2) Ghast Tear (0-1)

Friend/Foe	Found	Spawns	Armor	Health	Attack	Exp.	Drop
MAGMA CUBE	The Nether	Anywhere, often near Nether Fortresses	Big: 12 Small: 6 Tiny: 3	Big: 16 (8 Hearts) Small: 4 (2) Tiny: 1 (1/2)	Big: 6 Small: 4 Tiny: 3	5	Magma Cream (0-1, only Big and Small)

HOSTILE MOBS

Friend/Foe	Found	Spawns	Health	Attack	Exp.	Drop
BLAZE	The Nether (Nether Fortresses)	Light Level 11 or Less or Monster Spawners, both in Nether Fortresses	20 (10 Hearts)	Fireball- Easy: 3 Normal: 5 Hard: 7 Contact- Easy: 4 Normal: 6 Hard: 9	10	Blaze Rod (0-1) Glowstone (0-2)
ENDER DRAGON	The End	In The End	200 (100 Hearts)	Fireball- Easy: 6 Normal: 10 Hard: 15	12,000	Nothing

Friend/Foe	Found	Health	Attack	Exp.	Drop
ENDERMITE	Overworld (where Ender Pearls are thrown or where Endermen have teleported)	8 (4 hearts)	2	3	None
GUARDIAN	Overworld (Ocean Monuments)	30 (15 hearts)	Easy: 4 Normal: 6 Hard: 9 Defensive attack: 2	3	Prismarine Crystals Prismarine Shards Raw Fish Rare: Raw Fish Raw Salmon Blowfish Pufferfish
ELDER GUARDIAN	Overworld (Ocean Monuments)	80 (40 hearts)	Easy: 5 Normal: 8 Hard: 12 Defensive attack: 2	0	Prismarine Crystals Prismarine Shards Raw Fish Wet Sponge Rare: Raw Fish Raw Salmon Blowfish Pufferfish

HOSTILE MOBS

Friend/Foe	Found	Health	Attack	Exp.	Drop
WITHER SKELETON	Nether (Nether Fortresses)	20 (10 hearts)	Easy: 4 (Wither I effect) Normal: 7 (Wither I effect) Hard: 10 (Wither I effect)	5	Wither Skeleton Skull Stone sword Jack o'Lantern or Pumpkin (if during Halloween)
WITHER	Wherever the player builds it	300 (150 hearts)	Easy 5 Normal: 8 (Wither II effect) Hard: 12 (Wither II effect)	50	Nether Star
WITCH	Overworld (light levels of 7 or less, Witch Hut)	26 (13 hearts)	Potion of Slowness Potion of Poison (if player has 8 health left or more) Potion of Weakness Potion of Harming Defense: Potion of Water Breathing Potion of Fire Resistance Potion of Healing Potion of Swiftness 85% resistant to damage from magic	5	Glass Bottle Glowstone Dust Gunpowder Redstone Spider Eye Sugar Stick 1-3 drops or 0-2 items each

Villages often have farms.

NAVIGATION

If there's one thing that Minecraft is all about besides building, it's exploring, and this game does not slouch when it comes to giving you cool things to find. In fact, even a player that's plugged hundreds of hours into Minecraft can climb just one more mountain or break into just one more cavern and come across a gorgeous view that they've never seen in the game.

The world you see in Minecraft is essentially broken down into natural environments (Biomes) and environments spawned from building materials (Structures). In the Xbox 360 console version of Minecraft, there are currently four major Structures

and two minor Structures, each of which has its own rules for where it can occur, what type of creatures populate it and what can be found or done within it. Knowing this info can make a big difference in your gameplay, especially when attempting to survive at the beginning of a game or when looking for certain items later on. There's nothing like coming across a Chest of Diamond right when you need it!

Note: when exploring just about any of these, except the Village, you'll want to bring plenty of Torches or other items to mark your path, or you most definitely will get lost.

Village by night.

Villages are great places to find resources.

VILLAGES

If you're running around the Overworld (the part of the game that you spawn in), and you see a cluster of houses and think "Hey, I didn't build that!", you probably just found a Village. Villages are collections of buildings populated by neutral Villagers.

WHERE

Villages only spawn in Plains or Desert Biomes. They tend to spawn where it's flat, but they can also spawn on hills and across ravines, which can make for strange set-ups.

STRUCTURES

Depending on the available space, the game will place certain structures in a Village. The Hut, Butcher's Shop, Small House and Large House are simple structures made of Wood, Wood Planks and Cobble, and they usually contain a Villager or two. The Watch Tower and Church are taller structures with great views and a Villager, and you can also find Wells and Lamp Posts (made of one Black Wool block and some Torches). The most important Village structures, however, are the Farms, Library and Blacksmith, which contain useful items and in which Villagers live that can be traded with.

MOBS

The only mobs native to Villages are Villagers, baby Villagers and Iron Golems. Adult Villagers have professions and will breed with each other, and you can trade Emeralds with Villagers for various resources. You may also see Zombies attacking Villages in Zombie Sieges.

MATERIALS

Villages are excellent places to raid for building materials in a pinch, as they're made of things like Wood Planks and Cobblestone. The best resources, however, are found at the Farms, the Library and the Blacksmith. Farms yield Wheat and Wheat Seeds, which means you can easily make Bread or start your own Wheat Farm. Libraries contain Books (helpful for Enchanting) and a Crafting Table you can snatch up. The Blacksmith, however, has a couple Furnaces and the true treasure: a Chest of items. Check out the graph to the left to see what goodies you can expect in a Blacksmith's Chest.

A Stronghold library.

Beware of mobs in Strongholds.

STRONGHOLDS

At some point in the game, you'll either accidentally pop into one of these (often massive) structures, or you'll need to find one to get to The End. Strongholds can sometimes be small, but usually they're huge, confusing and highly dangerous. There are only three Strongholds per world.

WHERE

Find a Stronghold by throwing an Eye of Ender. The direction it flies toward is the direction of a Stronghold. If you don't have an Eye of Ender, you're going to have to just dig around until you crack into one. Strongholds are always at least 640 blocks from your start point and no farther than 1152, and they also often intersect sections like Ravines, Mineshafts and Caves.

STRUCTURES

Strongholds are mostly mazes of hallways, stairs and rooms, but they also include a few specific structures of note. These include Store Rooms, Libraries and the End Portal Room. Store Rooms are exactly what they sound like: an area that contains a Chest of useful stuff. Libraries are rooms full of Bookshelves and Cobwebs, and they come in one-story and two-story sizes. They also contain chests at the end of one or two bookshelves, depending on the size of the Library. The End Portal room is the only place in the world the player can get to The End, which is done by placing Eyes of Ender into the blocks of the End Portal, a structure that sits above a pool of Lava and is guarded by a Silverfish Monster Spawner.

MOBS

Fair warning: Strongholds are dangerous. They can contain just about every hostile mob in the Overworld, including Zombies, Skeletons, Spiders, Creepers and Silverfish. Silverfish are especially dangerous, as they can live in blocks called Monster Eggs that are disguised as normal blocks, and they attack in groups when one is damaged near others.

MATERIALS

Large parts of Strongholds are built out of materials that are hard to come by elsewhere, such as Iron Bars, Iron Doors, Buttons, and special Stone blocks like Mossy or Cracked Stone. Even better, the Chests in Strongholds carry some great items, with possibilities including Ender Pearls, Apples, Bread, Coal, Redstone, Armor, Iron Ingots, Iron Swords, Iron Pickaxes and, rarely, Diamond, Golden Apples or Saddles.

If you find an Abandoned Mineshaft, be ready for Cave Spiders.

Lucky players may find an Abandoned Mineshaft early and strip it of its Wood and other resources.

ABANDONED MINESHAFT

These are just what they sound like: mineshafts that spawn as if someone else had built them and then abandoned them.

WHERE
Randomly placed underground, especially intersecting with ravines and caves.

STRUCTURES
Mineshafts are simply hallways, stairways, crossings and rooms, often with Rail Tracks, supports and Minecarts in them.

MOBS
All mobs that can spawn in darkness have a chance of being in a Mineshaft, with the added danger of the smaller Cave Spider, which spawns from Monster Spawners and is unique to Abandoned Mineshafts. These little guys are poisonous, so watch out!

MATERIALS
If you plan on making anything out of Rails, breaking them up in Mineshafts is the most efficient method. Other simple materials such as Wood Planks, Fences and Torches can be found, as well as Chests, usually in Minecarts. See the chart at the left for likely Chest items.

Get ready to fight if you find a Dungeon.

DUNGEON

Small rooms randomly placed about the map, Dungeons contain a Monster Spawner and a Chest or two of items.

WHERE

Just about anywhere, but often in caves. Look for Mossy Stone and Cobblestone: those two together usually indicate a Dungeon.

STRUCTURES

Nothing more than one simple room!

MOBS

There will probably be tons of mobs of whatever type of Monster Spawner is in there (Zombie, Skeleton or Spider). Beware!

MATERIALS

Just Cobble and Mossy Stone and the Monster Spawner, besides what's in the Chest.

TEMPLES

Temples are awesome structures that look like big pyramids and which contain traps and Chests that contain useful items.

WHERE

Temples are only found in Jungles or in Deserts, and the two versions look slightly different from each other.

STRUCTURES

Both types of Temples are comprised of just one big building. Inside Jungle Temples, you'll find a puzzle that consists of three Levers and some Sticky Pistons. Desert Temples, on the other hand, have a secret room under a block of blue Wool. In the room is a trap consisting of a Stone Pressure Plate wired up to a large amount of TNT that will go off if the Plate is pressed. Also in the room will be 4 Chests with random loot from the same list as the Jungle Temple, making Desert Temples highly sought-after.

Nether Fortresses are not to be lightly trifled with.

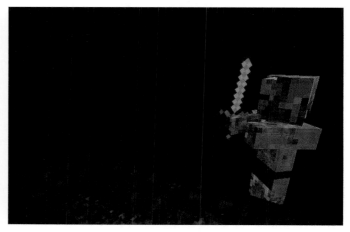

A Zombie Pigman stands guard over a crop of Nether Wart.

NETHER FORTRESSES

The only Structure found in the Nether, these are enormous, hugely dangerous and are the only place to find Nether Wart and Blazes. They're not too hard to find, but getting out alive requires great gear, patience and skill.

WHERE

The Nether, of course! Walk around long enough, and you're likely to find one, especially in big rooms, and when you do, the other Nether Forts will be laid out to the north and south in strips.

STRUCTURES

Nether Fortresses are comprised of tower-like structures connected by bridges. There are a few special rooms in the Forts: a stairwell with Nether Wart in it (the only place to find it), rooms with Blaze Spawners (also unique) and halls or rooms with Chests.

MOBS

You're most likely to come across Skeletons, Blazes and Magma Cubes in Nether Fortresses, while Ghasts may float above the bridges and Zombie Pigmen might be nearby. The rule for Nether Forts is to go in heavily armored and with the best weapons possible, as you will be attacked.

MATERIALS

Besides the Nether Brick they're made of, which is immune to Ghast fireballs, and the items that spawn in chests (Iron Ingots, Gold Ingots, Golden Chestplates and Swords, Saddles, Flint and Steel, Nether Wart and Diamonds are possible), Nether Forts are also the only place to get Blaze Rods (from killing Blazes) and Nether Wart, both of which are essential for crafting certain items (especially potions). You can also get Glowstone Dust from Blazes, occasionally.

OCEAN MONUMENTS

One of the newest additions to Minecraft in terms of things you can make a goal out of is the Ocean Monument, which is a very difficult to find and harder to conquer underwater temple of sorts. They're protected by dangerous Guardians and have many rooms, the top one of which is filled with Gold Blocks. A pretty nice reward!

WHERE

Ocean Monuments are found only in the Deep Ocean Biome. They're pretty tough to find because of both that and the fact that the math for where they spawn makes them not spawn very often. Also, if you started your world before the update with Ocean Monuments (September 2014), then they will ONLY spawn in Deep Ocean where you have not spent more than 3 minutes of game time. That means you might have to go searching for other Deep Ocean spots to find an Ocean Monument if you tend to hang out near one.

STRUCTURES

The Ocean Monument is one single, big structure, and we do mean big. Like most other structures, the Monument randomly generates according to rules, so it can be different sizes. It will always have at least six rooms inside with a central shaft that goes up to the "penthouse" with the treasure chamber, and it will also have two wings on either side of it. The treasure chamber and both wings feature a tough Elder Guardian, and the whole of the place is lit by Sea Lamps. You can also find rooms with a bunch of Wet Sponges in many of the Monuments. To get to Ocean Monuments and stay alive, you're

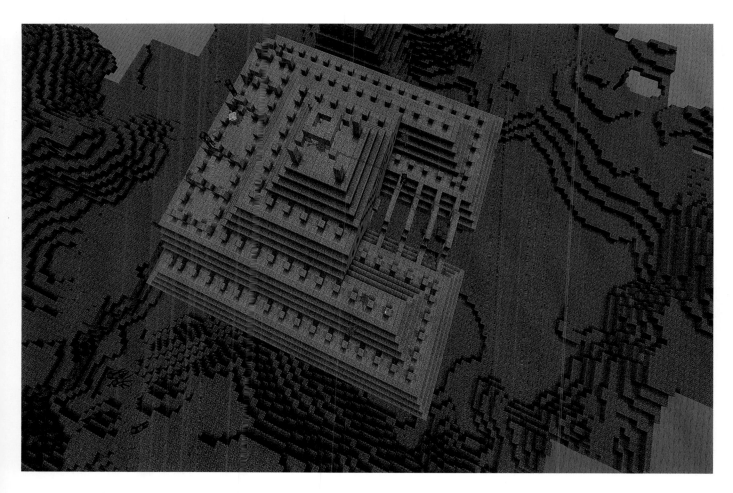

going to need to use Potions of Water Breathing, and probably a lot of other strong gear like heavy armor and weapons.

MOBS

The Guardian and the Elder Guardian are special mobs that only spawn in and around Ocean Monuments. Regular Guardians have a small chance of spawning outside of the Monument, but mostly will be inside, and Elder Guardians always spawn with one in each wing and one in the penthouse. They'll drop Raw Fish, Prismarine or Prismarine Shards sometimes, and have a ve y small chance of dropping another kind of fish.

These guys are tough and will go right at any player, attacking immediately with their laser that does three whole hearts of damage or their one heart-dealing spike defense. One good thing about the Guardians is that they will stop chasing the player if they lose sight of them, which you can use to your advantage.

Elder Guardians are much the same as Guardians but bigger, with a four heart attack, and they don't move as much. They also can inflict the "mining fatigue" status effect, which slows the player by 30% and makes breaking blocks slower. This is done without even touching the player once a minute if within 50 blocks of an Elder Guardian, and you'll see a ghostly form of the Guardian and a weird noise when it happens.

MATERIALS

Besides the Gold Blocks in the treasure room, the Ocean Monument is made out of different types of the material Prismarine. Prismarine is only used as a construction material (you can make Prismarine Bricks or Dark Prismarine from it) except you can also make Sea Lamps from it.

MINING BETTER

When it's time to slam a Pickaxe into some Stone, you need to be ready to go. There's gonna be a lot going on out there in your mine, from caves to explore, to mobs that'll attack you, to ore to snag and more, and it's easy to get distracted (and killed). Remember miner: when you put Pickaxe into hand and you set out for ore, you've got one goal, and that's to mine as well as you darn can.

To do that, you need to do three things: find resources, extract them, and return them to be stored in a safe area in as large amounts as is possible and as fast as is possible without dying.

To do that more often than you end up dead and far from your base, you need to keep a few things in mind.

All you need to mine is a good bit of Stone.

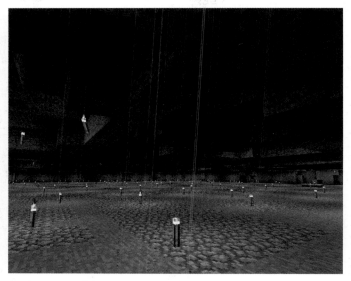

And soon you'll have something like this.

MINING

Mining is broken down into two types: clearing an area, and ore mining.

CLEARING AN AREA MINING

Just like it sounds, this is when you're not necessarily looking for ore; you're mainly trying to clear a space for a shelter or some other reason. This is fairly straightforward, but there are some ideas that can help you do this quickly and more efficiently:

- As always, don't dig straight up or straight down. This is the time when players are most likely to do this, so it's worth repeating.

- Cut out the shape of the thing you're making first. Designing a good area works best when you make sure of the dimensions before you start the heavy digging. Just mine out the outline of what you want to build and the rest will go much quicker.

- You can mine 4 blocks forward and 3 down from the one you're standing on without moving. Mining as much as you can in a straight line makes for more efficient mining.

- Stay aware. You never know when you might crack into a cave, Stronghold or Lava pit. Be ready.

- Take the ore you see. Don't let the plan keep you from grabbing some ore. Get ore as soon as you see it, then replace the blocks if you need to keep a certain shape going.

- Create stopgaps with Doors. Don't just mine open tunnels all the time. Put Doors in and even create little mini-bases, and you'll mine much safer and faster.

Some gold in a cave.

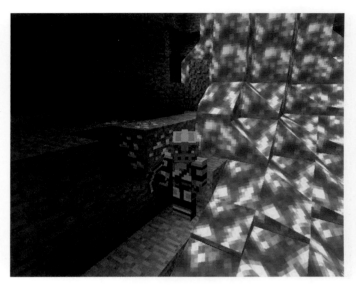

A proud miner stands by his Diamonds.

ORE MINING

This is the big one, guys. Ore is essential to Minecraft. Ore is what you want, what you need and what you will get if you try hard and have a little luck.

The Basic Idea: You're looking for ore deposits, and all ore is created right when you start your world. It's placed around your world according to certain rules and algorithms, and there are places it won't spawn, places it might spawn and places it's likely to spawn. Each ore is different. You need to know where each ore spawns and then look for it in those places.

Basic Techniques: Beyond just rushing into a big, beautiful pile of stone and hacking away at it with a Pickaxe, you should prepare yourself and have at least some idea of a plan before you go charging in. Try these techniques.

Prepare your inventory. Make sure you have most of your inventory clear, but you need to bring a few things for even basic mining.

Ore	Best Layers to Find On	General Layer Range	No Ore On or Above This Layer
Coal	5-52	5-128	132
Iron	5-54	5-64	68
Gold	5-29	5-29	34
Redstone	5-12	5-12	16
Diamond	5-12	5-12	16
Lapis Lazuli	14-16	5-23	34
Emerald	5-29	5-29	33
Nether Quartz (Nether only)	15-120	5-120	126

NOTE: Layer counting starts at the Bedrock as Layer 1

You will find mobs in your mines. Be ready.

This mineshaft cracked right into the End Portal room of a Stronghold.

Bringing much more is not recommended, as you'll need your inventory full for things you pick up/mine.

- Plan out the location and length of your excursion. If you're looking for a certain ore, you know that you'll need to go to the level it spawns in. If you're mining close to home, keep in mind where your existing structures are so that you don't accidentally run a mineshaft into one. If you're going out to a new cave or area, make sure you know or mark the way back.

- Keep it tidy. It might seem like a hassle while you're doing it but trust us; when you go back to an area you've already mined, and you didn't keep the excavation tidy and easily understood, you'll wish you had. You'll get a lot more out of mining if you clean up and light your tunnels as you go instead of leaving them dark and confusing. Make signs if you have to!

- Watch out for mobs. They spawn in the dark, and they will get you if you're not paying attention.

- If you break into or come across a big, new area, mark the entrance to your existing mine as much as possible. Light that thing up with Torches, because it is very easy to forget the way back.

A completed staircase to the Bedrock.

Staircase in progress.

ADVANCED TECHNIQUES

Once you've got the hang of basic mining, try some of these tried-and-true methods for ultra-efficient ore discovery.

THE STAIRCASE METHOD:

Most veteran Minecrafters will tell you that this is one of the best and most common methods for quick ore discovery, and it's easy to do. All you do is create a staircase from where you start mining all the way to the bedrock. Some players prefer a straight diagonal staircase, while others go for a spiral; either is fine. You may crack into a tunnel, cave or even a Stronghold on the way. If you can, mark this and keep digging your staircase until it's finished. If you can't (say, you crack into the top of a ravine), start a new staircase instead of trying to move this one over. The reason for all of this is that it greatly simplifies mining at deeper levels. If you have a staircase that accesses every level, you can head directly to the level you need depending on the ore you're looking for. Plus, it's very easy to see where you've already explored and to start in on a new area by building staircases this way.

The results of branch mining: Diamonds!

The branch mining hallway grows.

A branch.

BRANCH MINING:

Combined with the Staircase Method, branch mining is the simplest way to hugely increase your chances at finding good ore. It's also fairly easy, yay! To branch mine, pick a level at which the ores you want can be found. Typically this is layer 15 and below. When there, mine out a hallway 2 blocks wide and 3 blocks tall. Make this as long as you want, just make sure it goes straight. When you've got a decently long hall, go back to the front. Now, aim at one of the first blocks on the wall of the hall and mine a new hall (the branch hall) perpendicular to the original hall. This new branch hall should be only 1 block wide and 3 blocks tall. Mine it back about 7-12 blocks, then put a Torch at the end. Go back along the new hall and mine out any ores you find, then go back to the main hall. Looking at your new 1 block wide branch hall, move to the right 2 blocks, and make another 1 block wide branch hall off of the main hall, going back the same amount of blocks and taking any ore you find. Repeat this process on both sides of the main hall until you reach the end, then either extend the main hall and repeat or start a new one somewhere else. What this does is to reveal the most blocks with the least digging, meaning you're more likely to see ore with less work and time put in.

THE CAMP

Perhaps the best habit you can adopt for yourself as a miner is to never mine far from a base. This doesn't mean you need to stay by your home, far from it. We just mean that if you're mining and there isn't a Chest or five, a Crafting Table, a Furnace, maybe a Bed and certainly some safe, safe walls to get to quickly, you're mining dangerously.

Mining free, with a base farther than a minute or so away, is a fine tactic when you're out exploring, just starting a world or otherwise unable to invest any large amount of time into the effort, but once you've established a home, you should rarely be mining without having a secure area nearby in which to resupply, deposit gathered resources and hide from the elements.

Camps can be built just about anywhere, as all you need to do is build a small room wherever you are. Don't hesitate to wall off a section of a cave or build a safehouse within a structure like a ravine, Fortress or any other. You have mastery over this land, if you'll take it, and you can never really have enough safehouses.

To produce the best results, plan your mines by first picking a good spot for a mining camp/safehouse, such as at the bottom of a deep staircase, or built up in a natural structure such as a ravine or cave. Bring the stuff you'll need to build a good camp along with you to the spot you want to mine before actually mining, and it will make your ore collection progress much quicker than it otherwise would.

Well-lit tunnels are a must for any good camp.

Another shot of a good mining camp, complete with Chests, a Crafting Table and a furnace.

Camps can be as elaborate or simple as you'd like, but each should meet a few requirements: they should be secure from mobs (meaning they should be well-lit and only accessible through Doors or Trapdoors), they should be easily accessible from your mine (no more than a minute or two away from where you're mining), and they should contain a Chest with helpful items, a Crafting Table, a Furnace and possibly a Bed at the least.

Good items to bring to start a base include Wood of any kind (as well as Planks and Sticks), Cobblestone, tools and weapons, food, and Coal, Charcoal and Torches. Unless you expand your mining camps into more permanent bases, you should think of them as places to resupply and work temporarily, so transport rare or valuable items back to your main bases when you can.

This Miner has all the gear he needs to set out in search of ore.

Don't forget the Armor and the Sword when you go minin'!

For Mining

3 or 4 Stone Pickaxes

2 or 3 Stone Shovels

At least 2 Pickaxes of higher quality

At least 1 Shovel of higher quality

1 full stack of Torches or more
(4 stacks is a good number)

Enough food to get full from empty three times
(cooked meat and Bread are great options)

1 full stack of Cobblestone, 2 at most (partially
in order to make a Furnace)

Whatever Wood you can spare (a full stack of
Wood is ideal, but at least some Wood, Wood
Planks and/or Wood Sticks is a very good idea)

When First Setting Up Base Add

As many Torches as you can

As much Coal as you can

As much Wood as you can

3 more Shovels and Pickaxes of any type
except Wood or Gold

2 or more Chests

1 Crafting Table

Some Iron Ore or Iron Ingots

THE GEAR

A Pickaxe is all you need to mine, but it's not the only item you should take with you on your trips. When you need to mine, plan an extensive mining excursion that takes a bit of time and gear, and your trips will be much more rewarding.

Miners out on a serious resource acquiring jaunt should take as much of the kit to the left as possible for best results. You might not be able to acquire all of this gear at first, so just take as much as you can and improve your kit as you expand. Eventually, you'll be able to add to this kit and outdo it by adding better items as you progress in your world.

Each time you go out on a planned trip to mine, take the mining kit with you, and stay out mining until you use it all up or run out of inventory space. By doing this and combining it with the practices that follow, you'll end up with the maximum number of resources in the least amount of time.

THE EXPLORATORY TRIPS

As tempting as it might be, don't go just randomly mining when you find a cave or other structure (or at least don't do so for long). Plan your trips, get your gear ready, know where your base is, and head out with an area in mind.

- The best mines are centered around a mineshaft (a vertical shaft with a ladder) or a staircase that goes from ground level to the bedrock. Build tunnels or clear out levels around these, never going too far from the center staircase or mineshaft and always going straight out from the center. No twisting passages or changing levels, just straight halls, rooms and tunnels with flat floors.

- Keep your mine organized, but also collect all resources you see. When you find ore, follow it and mine it all out, but when it's done, repair your mine so that you keep it easy to understand. For instance, if you come across some ore that goes below the level that the rest of your mine is on, mine it out and then replace the floor so that it stays flat.

- Remember the two rules of ore finding: ore is most common below level 16 and near Lava. If you're really looking for ore, you want to have a base in the lower levels so you can explore them, and you want to look out for Lava. When you find Lava, dig around it, containing it as you go, and you'll more than likely come across some nice resource deposits.

BEST MINING PRACTICES

Some general tips for mining, these will refine your tactics into well-developed, highly efficient processes.

- Use tools to breaking. You're already out, and though you might have some other project you feel like rushing off to, you're best served by using up the tools you have when you're already in your mine. If you take our mining kit with you and use it all up, you'll collect more resources each time you're out, making the time you spent in your mine much more worthwhile.

- Your mine should have a straight shot to the surface. We've covered this a bit before, but it bears reiteration, as it's so key to good mining. It should never be hard to get back to the surface from your mine, and if it is, you should make an easy exit for yourself.

- You should have a quick shot back to base when mining as well. Again, we've covered this but we're going to say it again: it should never take more than a minute or two to get back to a base from where you're mining. Keep mining far away from base and we can tell you from experience that a Creeper's gonna find you and ruin your day sooner than later.

- Deposit resources often. It's a guaranteed win when you take your resources back to your secure base no matter how little or how much you've gathered. Do it as much as possible.

- Leave no dark spots in your mines. No matter how small the shadowy spots are in your mine, light them up. You should never, ever have mobs spawning in the areas you are mining, and you can make that happen by using Torches and other light sources liberally.

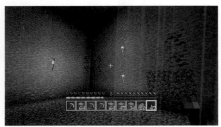

· Use signs to direct yourself. Whether it's telling you what level you're on or that a cave or base is "This Way," use signs. There's never going to be a moment where you are sad that a sign told you where something is, and there will be many times you wish there was one to help out.

· Keep your tools close together in your tray. Switching between tools like Pickaxes and Shovels can take up a lot of time over many switches, so keep them right next to each other and you'll save a lot of minutes.

· Go in pairs, with one player mining and the other organizing. If playing multiplayer, split the responsibilities by having one player expand the mine and gather resources while the other cleans up behind them and keeps the mine organized. It really is worth the trouble.

· Leave a third of your Iron tools by switching to Stone for mining lesser materials. Use your Iron tools on all materials until there's about a third of them left. Then switch to Stone tools unless you find something that requires Iron to break. This allows you to stay out longer, as you can still collect the more valuable ores while continuing to expand your mine.

COMBAT

Thing is, when you play Minecraft in Survival mode, some creature at some point in the game will attempt to kill you, and it will succeed. We all know this when we start a world (which typically involves dying once or five times), but after a while you get comfy in your safe house and well-lit mine, and you forget that outside your cozy walls lies death. And then it comes for you, in the form of a sizzling Creeper you didn't see until it was too late, or a nest of Cave Spiders that you suddenly crack into, and you're dead. All your gear is probably lost, you're far from where you were, and then you remember: combat happens in Minecraft. Let's get you ready to fight.

1. PREPARE FOR BATTLE, YOUNG MINER

Nothing you do in Minecraft is more important to your success in combat than preparation. Every good strategy involves at least some of it, and it is the core of almost all successful offense and defense. Fail to prepare, or at least think ahead a bit, and you're gonna die. Do even the smallest bit of prep work, and you're gonna kill some mobs, kiddo.

So let's get you prepared. These are far from the only ways to prepare in this game, but they'll at least get you set on the path to tasty triumph over the dark forces that wait outside the walls of your home.

Crafter Robot Noise is decked out in enchanted armor and a Diamond Sword, ready for battle.

You'll notice the difference that Diamond gear makes right away. There really is no substitute.

Eat This, Not That

Best before battle:
- Golden Apple
- Cooked Porkchop
- Steak

Good before battle:
- Cooked Chicken
- Mushroom Stew
- Bread
- Cooked Fish

Bad before battle:
- Apple
- Melon
- Uncooked meat
- Cookie

Light up the area around your base. Hostile mobs only spawn where the light level is low. When you leave your base unlit, you're letting the mobs choose when to fight you. Turn the tables by lighting the area around your base, that way you only fight on your terms.

It's okay to spend on gear. We know, we know— you want to save that Diamond. Well, we get that, but trust us on this one. The amount of lesser materials you will save by spending that Iron or Diamond on good Armor and weapons is going to make that enchanted Diamond Sword pay for itself. You won't just die less, you'll die a lot less, and your ability to kill mobs quickly will result in experience and drops galore.

A miner's gotta eat. Food is the most often forgotten and perhaps most important part of combat. Health regeneration and the ability to sprint (and thus knock the mob back, aka "knockback") depend on your continuing to have a full food bar (the bar with the meat-on-bones). Eat foods that have good hunger-to-saturation restoration levels before battle for best effects, and avoid those with low hunger-to-sat. You should also bring such foods with you when going out hunting and eat them whenever hungry. Keeping yourself well-fed with the right foods all throughout your combat period is essential.

Screenshot: Minecraft® ™ & © 2009–2015 Mojang/Notch.

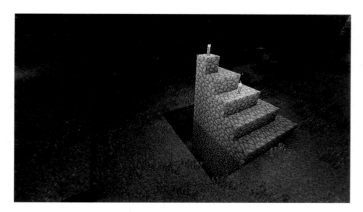

This pit and staircase combo is an excellent build for mob hunting, as it allows you to shoot from on top of it, drawing mobs toward you and hopefully into the pit. Make it even better by building a fence and a gate at the back.

Prepare the land. Make the battlefield your own, not just with lights, but with traps, murder holes and more. The thrill of attacking blind is great at times, but if you're looking to become a true hunter, take the daylight hours to prepare your hunting grounds for maximum success. Create pits, holes and cliffs to lead or knock mobs into and know where they are. Build tunnels and places to attack from above (little towers and forts) that you can access but keep you safe from mobs. This is where you can start to have the most fun with hunting (and essentially farming) mobs, and where you can get the most creative. Turn the area around your base into a place that invites mobs in, murders them brutally and leaves the spoils for you to collect.

2. OFFENSE IS THE BEST OFFENSE

When combat comes, and it will, don't go swinging blindly. And in fact, don't just swing. The Minecraft community has come up with a few tried and true methods that will amplify your ability to come out of a mob encounter on the life-having end by enormous amounts, and you'll find they'll lead to a lot fewer frantic trips back to your dropped pile of loot.

Sprint and hit to get a knockback. Attacking a mob at sprint causes you to knock it back. This is good for two reasons: It puts distance between you and the mob, and it gives you the opportunity to knock them off of something and damage them. This is especially useful when you know or have prepared the battleground.

Circle around while attacking: the circle strafe. One of Minecraft's two most trusted attack styles, circle strafing involves putting an enemy in the center of your vision while you walk around them in a circle, attacking the whole time. Called the circle strafe, this method makes it hard for most enemies to attack while giving you the opportunity to do damage. **NOTE: does not work on Creepers unless you're just crazy good at it.**

Flint & Steel Is, in fact, so useful in combat that it should be considered second most essential to a Sword.

Attack, pull back and draw them in, attack again: Kiting. Kiting is the second of the two sacred Minecraft combat strategies. "Kiting a mob" is when you hit a mob and then back away while keeping your vision focused on the mob. Mobs immediately attack after you hit them, so by pulling away, you can direct them toward you (as if you were pulling them on a kite string). As your target comes to attack, time a second attack perfectly so that they are hit and knocked back a bit, giving you the chance to back away again and repeat the process. Kiting is one of the safer and most effective strategies in Minecraft combat, and it can be used in combination with archery as well as with traps for seriously damaging attacks.

- **Swords aren't your only weapons.** The best hunters use all of their tools. Swords are the primary weapon, but you can also light blocks on fire with Flint and Steel, drop Lava, suffocate with Gravel or Sand (you have to time those just right), drown with Water and even slow mobs down with Cobwebs or Soulsand. Try all of these in combat at least once and arm yourself with the weapons you are best at using.

3. KEEPING ALIVE: DEFENSE IN MINECRAFT

While prepping and attacking correctly are great, sometimes you just need to stay alive to win the fight. And, let's be honest, sometimes you just need to stay alive period. Don't let your first thirty deaths get ya down, Crafters: staying alive can be done, and done well.

Putting a wall between the Crafter and the Creeper will save you over and over.

Putting Torches down while attacking ensures that mobs won't spawn in this exact area again (though they might be able to travel there).

This angry Spider can't get to his attacker when he's underwater!

Use the zigzag method. Most mobs do not do well with direction change when it comes to attacking (the Silverfish being a definite exception). Skeletons in particular just can't handle it, so whether you're attacking or running away, strafing from side to side will boost your chances of success.

Put blocks between you and them. Mobs will chase you, but if you make a move when they can't see you, they won't know you did it. This means that getting behind something and then changing direction or tactics can save your butt more often than not. This is great for attacking, but even better when you need to get yourself out of combat quickly.

Go underwater. No mob can swim to try and kill you underwater, so if you need to get away, dive down, kid.

Spam those Torches. Remember, mobs will keep spawning anywhere there is darkness, and if mobs have put you in a bad situation in one spot on the map once, they probably will do so again unless you do something. Spamming Torches on the environment when running is a great preventative measure for now and the future.

Any good general will tell you: always take the higher ground when possible.

With full health, this Zombie should be no problem. If this Miner was hurtin', however, it would be best to avoid combat in this dark tunnel.

4. GENERALLY GOOD IDEAS

Just plain smart things to think about when it comes to Minecraft huntin'.

Creepers start their countdown when you are within three blocks and end it when you leave the three block range. That might sound like pretty specific advice, but anyone who's played the game much at all knows that no other mob really compares to the Creeper when it comes to doin' damage. Know this fact and use it to your advantage.

Don't fight unless you can and want to. You don't have to prove your bravery in Minecraft. Fighting when you are close to death, don't have good gear, are far from home or are otherwise unprepared leads to death, which leads to losing precious items and time. Run away first, fight when the odds are in your favor, and your game will progress a whole lot faster than that of your "brave" friends.

5. COLONEL CREEPERKILLER'S STRATEGY CORNER

Okay we made that name up, but this neat little strategy section needed a flashy title. Pulled from the deep depths of the Crafter community, these specific strategies should be learned and used when you find yourself in a tough spot. When you get good at them all and combine them with the above tips, you'll find yourself wrecking your way through wave after endless wave of mobs, reaping their delicious experience orbs and laughing as you stand tall as the apex predator of the Minecraft world. Or something like that. NOTE: These tricks can be used on mobs or, if you're feeling rascally, on other players.

By digging above this Zombie, he has no idea he's about to die.

Getting past mobs in tunnels is a great use of the Ender Pearl (if you can afford to use one).

When a Creeper's coming head-on like this, the best option is to get around him and hit from behind.

The Duck and Swing. Best on mobs, make the mob lose sight of you, then move to attack mode. Basically, move to a place where the mob can't see you. They will continue to come at the last place they saw you, so you can move yourself to a place where you can attack them. Swing around behind or above, and you'll have the advantage on the unsuspecting mob. This strategy is super tricky in PvP, but it feels pretty great when you pull it off.

The Reverse Sapper. Tunnel above enemies or mobs and unleash your fury. Don't feel confined to the way the environment is set up. If you know where they'll be, dig so that you pop up just above them and rock them with attacks. One of the most effective strategies there is.

Ender Bouncing. Pretty straightforward, but expensive: throw Enderpearls to teleport around the battlefield. Especially effective when you throw them through throw walls of fire or where enemies can't see/reach, gaining you a tactical advantage.

A Creeper's about to learn what the Pit Knock is.

The Mini Murder Fort from a distance.

Stack your Mini Murder Fort with some useful items.

Finn Fu done correctly is devastating.

The hilarious Sato Technique about to make a Creeper pay.

The Pit Knock. Set up a pit that's either deep enough to damage anything that falls in it or that has something damaging in it like Cactus or fire. Lure enemies near it and knock 'em in with a sprint attack or a weapon with the Knockback enchantment. Mob falls in, collect loot at the bottom, profit. Can also be made more complicated by creating a drowning or suffocating trap (see the Inventions section).

The Murder Hole. Create a border around a part of your base where you leave one block open just above where the ground level is on the outside of the base. On the inside of the base, make this spot accessible so that it is at your head-height. This will make it so you can attack the feet of mobs, while most can't get to you. Spiders, however, still sometimes can. Stinkin' Spiders.

The Mini Murder Fort. Get yourself all geared up and find a good spot out in the wild during the day where mobs are likely to spawn at night. Build yourself a little spot where you can reach mobs on all sides but they have a hard time getting to you. This can either be slightly up in the air or slightly underground (or both, for The Ultra Mini Murder Fort), putting you just out of reach of most mobs. Wait til dark, and then wreck all that dare come near. Even Spiders will usually just jump on top, and if you have a one-block hole punched in the ceiling, you'll have a fine window to kill them through.

Finn Fu. Start a ranged attack on an enemy with a Bow, then create a large firewall on a line of blocks in front of you using Flint and Steel. The enemy can't see through the fire, so drop TNT blocks behind it. Pull away from the firewall, shooting through it at the enemy. If hit, the enemy will usually kite, following you through the firewall. This will light them on fire, running them into the TNT and blowing them up. Works even better if you can put it in a pit and then escape out of the top of it. NOTE: Most items and blocks are destroyed by TNT. You will probably still find some resources that were hit with the shock-wave, however.

The Sato Technique. Set a TNT trap by digging down two blocks and placing one TNT block at the bottom of the pit. Put a block that can take a Pressure Plate above the TNT and put a Pressure Plate on it. Now kite a mob or enemy over the plate, and if you can keep them in the general vicinity, they'll go sky-high when the TNT detonates. Also works best in a pit. NOTE: Also destroys most items. But is really, really funny. Can also be used as a trap around your base, but not too close of course (unless you've got an Obsidian blast wall).

FARMING & ADVANCED AGRICULTURE

Runnin' around and a'murderin' mobs in order to get food, or making maniacal runs on Villager Wheat farms, is all well and good, and will get you through the beginning of the game just fine. However, later in the game, having to leave your base for food trips can get exceedingly tedious and frustrating, and it usually leads to a cycle of taking quick hunting trips that never gather enough food, leading you have to go huntin' again not too far in the future.

In the end, having a ready food source built into your home such as a farm or ranch is almost a must for a Minecrafter, and they really aren't too hard to set up. Here are the basics of farming, plus a few ways to kick your virtual food acquisition game into high gear.

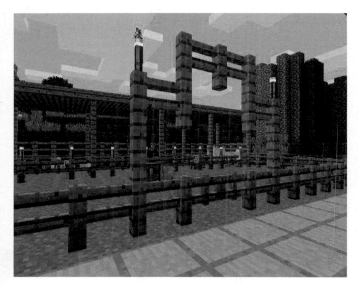

The Tutorial world has a great example of an animal farm.

Sheep: they love Wheat.

FARMING

Farming also has two distinctive types. One revolves around the capture of animals to breed and harvest meat and drops from, and the other revolves around planting and harvesting crops of plants.

ANIMAL FARMING

Don't worry, this isn't about to get all Orwellian. Animal farming is pretty simple in Minecraft, though some automated breeder inventions can take things to a whole 'nother level. What you need to do for an animal farm is fourfold: find the animals and get them to follow you, put them in an enclosure, breed them and then harvest them.

1. Find and Follow: Most peaceful animal mobs in Minecraft have a certain item that they really like, and when you hold it, they'll follow you. This is ultra-convenient for animal farming, as otherwise you have to shove animals one by one into your pens, or just hope they walk in on their own. Here's what animal follows what item:

- Wheat: Cows, Pigs, Sheep and Mooshrooms
- Wheat Seeds: Chickens
- Bone (use on to tame): Wolves

You can tell that animals are ready to breed when they display the floating hearts.

A Baby Cow!

2. Put 'em in a Pen: Now that you've got some animals following, you need a place to put them. If you haven't built one already, just stick them in your home and close the door for now. Building pens is what Fences were made for, and this is where you should use 'em. Mobs need to be pretty close to each other to ensure breeding, so make a pen for each type of mob, and make them pretty small (maybe 8x8 at the largest, but more often smaller). Use Gates on each pen in order to get in and out, and remember that some mobs are hard to get in through a 1 block wide hole, so make double Gates if necessary. It's also a good idea to put all the pens near each other, and then fence around the entire section of pens. This makes it less likely that any mobs will get out, and it gives you a space to let some roam a bit if you need to do so.

3. Breed those Guys: Breeding is a necessity for any good farm because it allows you to turn your animals into renewable resources. There's not a lot of point in going out and collecting animals just to kill them, and then have to do it again, right? To breed animals, you simply need to find the right item to feed them, then feed two of them in the same area. They'll find each other, breed, and a new little baby animal will spawn!

Here's what each animal needs to breed:
- Wheat: Cows, Pigs, Sheep, Mooshrooms
- Any seed (not just Wheat Seeds): Chicken
- Any meat: Tamed Wolves
- Raw Fish: Ocelots/Cats

4. Time for the Harvest: Yes, they may be cute when they're bouncing around in your pens, but you need that food! To harvest meat and items from animals, simply kill them. You can light them on fire to kill them and have their meat drop already cooked (if they drop meat), but this method doesn't drop experience. Use a Sword, and take a few out. The key here is to make sure you leave at least two animals of each species alive so that they can keep breeding later. A note: there's no reason to kill Tamed Wolves. They don't drop any items, and besides, they're your friends!

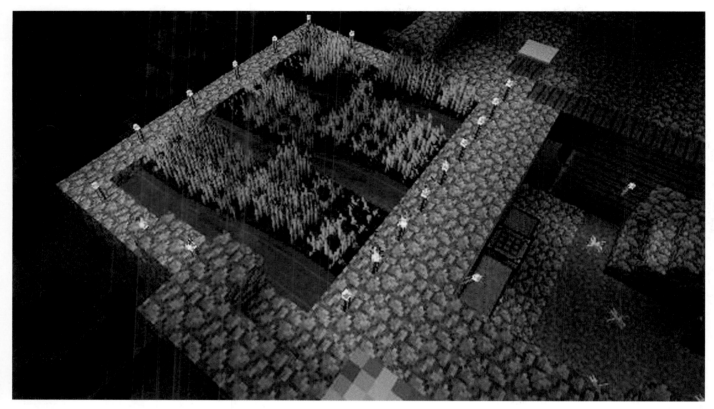

A cool-lookin' farm on the side of a castle.

PLANT FARMING

The primary plants for farming in Minecraft are Wheat, trees, and Pumpkins and Melons. You can also farm Sugar Cane, Mushrooms, Nether Wart and Cactus, but these are the plants that you're most likely to need and to farm in your game.

Wheat Farms: Wheat is probably the most commonly farmed plant (it's between Wheat and trees), and it's simple to farm. Wheat requires a light level of 9 or above and what's called farmland, which is what a block of Dirt turns into when you use a Hoe on it. For best Wheat growth, it should be no more than 4 blocks from a source of Water as well. Wheat takes a variable amount of time to grow, but grows fastest under conditions where it's well-lit and on hydrated farmland. Harvested Wheat drops

0-3 Wheat Seeds when cut, making it a renewable resource. Use Torches or Glowstone near Wheat in order to make it grow even without sunlight.

Tree Farms: Wood is a hugely important resource in Minecraft, so tree farms can make your virtual life a lot easier. Like Wheat, trees need light, but they don't need Water to grow, so again use Torches to grow trees. The easiest tree to grow is the Oak, and the easiest way to grow it is to make a 5x5x2 space of Dirt. In each corner, dig a hole 1 block down and plant an Oak Sapling in each hole. Put 3 Torches to a side, and the trees will grow easily. Trees usually drop Saplings, making it easy to replace them.

Wheat, Melons and Pumpkins need Water and farmland.

Set up your farm in this pattern.

Melon/Pumpkin Farming: Pumpkins and Melons are both farmed in the same way. Pumpkins and Melons work best on farmland with hydration, like Wheat, but they grow differently. When planted, their seeds make a stem, which when mature grows a Melon or Pumpkin in one of the 4 adjacent blocks. This means you need to leave at least one space and preferably more around a planted Pumpkin or Melon Seed. These also produce Seeds when harvested.

You can build an advanced farm by building it in tiers. By building the same shape of farm one on top of the next (leaving a little space between for movement and lighting it up with Torches, of course). You only need one source of Water if you let it flow down from one to the next!

TWO STYLES OF AUTOMATED FARMS

Piston Farms can easily be attached to most existing farms.

THE PISTON FARMER

Pistons are one of the most dynamic and useful objects in the Minecraft universe, and when it comes to farming, they can help you out quite a lot. This build takes advantage of the fact that an activated Piston that shoves over a plot of grown Wheat will cause the Wheat to break and drop so you can grab it and use it.

This build can be added to most farms, but you'll need to leave at least one or two blocks next to each block where you will grow Wheat. All you need to do then is place a Piston on the empty block one block next to and one block above the block on which you're growing the Wheat. Make sure the Piston faces the Wheat, and do this for every block where there will be Wheat. Then, wire all of the Pistons together with Redstone so that they lead to one single Lever. (You may need some Repeaters.)

The Water Scythe caught in action as it harvests Wheat for you.

When you flip the Lever, all Pistons should extend across where the Wheat has grown, breaking the Wheat. Flip the Lever again so that the Pistons detract, and where there once was a Wheat farm, there is now a large amount of Wheat icons floating on empty patches of Dirt, and you can just run down your farm and grab them, replanting as you go.

THE WATER SCYTHE

Piston farming's fun, but when it comes to efficiency, nothing beats the Water Scythe. Like Pistons, Water that flows over a block of growing Wheat will break it. Unlike Pistons, however, flowing Water will actually carry the dropped Wheat with it.

By using both of these features, we can harvest an entire farm with the flick of a Lever and direct the flow of the Water so that all of the harvested Wheat gathers in one spot for you to pick up.

For this, you'll want to build your farm in a terrace formation, with one level of the farm one block below the other. Before you plant, go to the far end of the top level of your farm, and build a little wall with alcoves (holes) in it that line up with where the Wheat will be planted. Now, place Buckets of Water in the alcoves so that it flows out over the whole farmland, making sure that it doesn't overflow the sides. Test this out a bit so that you get it right.

Now move to the bottom level of your farm and see where the Water is flowing out. Build around this so that all of the Water collects in one trench that goes downhill and ends in one single block (without overflowing).

Go back to the top of your farm and temporarily remove the Water. What you need to do now is control when the Water comes out. The best way to do this is by building a system of Sticky Pistons, blocks and a Lever, so that when you push the Lever, the Pistons remove the blocks from in front of the Water, allowing it to flow (and when you push it again, the Pistons put the blocks back and stop the Water). If you don't have or don't want to use Sticky Pistons, however, you can simply use a block of Dirt over the alcove that you punch out when you want to harvest your Wheat.

Once it's all set up, plant your Wheat and wait until harvest day, which will be the easiest one you've ever had.

WHAT TO DO WHEN

There's a moment in just about every long-haul Crafting session where you come up against something tough, and you're just not sure what to do about it. Minecraft is full of these kind of moments, whether it's deciding to stay down in your mine for another fifteen minutes before heading back to base, or whether you suddenly find yourself in peril and aren't sure if you should fight, fly or just throw in the towel and reload from your last save. While there are really no wrong answers in this game that's all about experimentation and playing how you like, there are some tips for certain situations that we can give you that can make your next mining trip go a bit smoother (by which we mean less full of death and woe).

1. YOU'RE LOST AND CAN'T FIND HOME (OR ANYTHING ELSE YOU RECOGNIZE).

We all love the goofy, blocky graphics of Minecraft, but we also have to admit that they can make it hard to keep your sense of direction. Since there are only so many types of blocks and environments, you can quickly get turned around both above and below ground. If you're stuck out in the wild and are starting to think you'll never see home again, try these tips.

- Get up high. If you're above ground, create a Dirt tower so you can look out over a bigger area, or climb a tree. If you're underground, stop trying to find your way out naturally and just dig up in a staircase pattern. Moving up is almost always beneficial in Minecraft when lost or stuck, and you can always go back down if you need to!

- Mark your path. Always, always mark your path, especially when you're already lost. Use towers, Torches, just about anything you'll recognize, and you'll start to weed out all the wrong directions (and will stop going in circles, as can definitely happen).

- Use the Cobblestone/Nether Rack "north" trick. If you look at blocks of either of these, you'll see that they have an "L" shape on the texture (on the regular texture pack). If you situate your miner so that the L is facing the correct direction (meaning it looks like the letter should), you are facing north.

Spawn Spider

2. YOU'RE STUCK OUTSIDE/UNDERGROUND WITHOUT RESOURCES AND MOBS ARE ABOUT.

Mobs don't care if you're ready for combat or not: they're coming for you. It's pretty likely that you're gonna find yourself in a bad spot at some point, with mobs a'comin' and no Sword, Bow or other weapons to speak of. What do you do?

- Get up high. Like with being lost, getting off the ground level is an excellent combat measure. Mobs have a hard time climbing even one block and most can't climb two (just Spiders), so put some air between you and your foes.

- Run straight through. Sometimes the best way to survive is to just put on a burst of speed and try and break through the line of mobs. If possible, eat something before you do this.

- Protect your resources. It's always easier to come back and find a Chest with items in it than it is to rush back to get the gear that dropped when you died. Bring Chests with you when you mine and store all of your important stuff when in a bad spot before trying to escape.

- If possible, build a mini-mini murder fort. Obviously you don't have time to do any major construction, but if you can surround yourself with blocks and leave just a little space to attack through, you should be able to time it so that you can hit mobs and they can't reach you. Very effective in a pinch.

3. THERE'S A CREEPER IN YOUR HOME (OR PROJECT, OR MINE, ETC.).

It happens, sometimes a lot, and it's terrifying. There's one thing to do.

- Get out. Immediately. It's the Creeper's home now. Okay, not really to that last bit, but seriously, just go. While you might be able to kill the thing, there's just too much at risk. Unless you don't care what happens to the place, it's always better to leave and let the creepy thing see itself out or despawn than it is to risk having to put half your house back together.

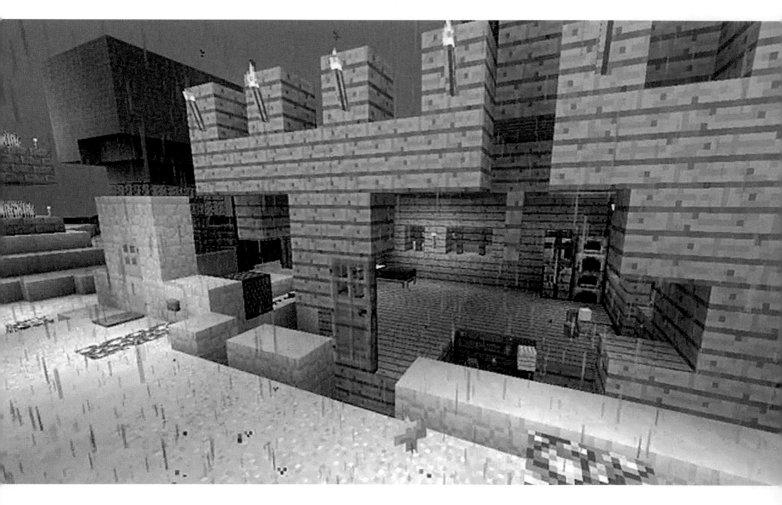

4. A CREEPER DONE BLEW UP YOUR HOME.

But of course, sometimes you just can't get away in time. Creepers do be creepin'. But don't panic; you have options.

- Consider reloading. It may seem cheap, but so is showing up unannounced, sneaking right next to you and your beloved project and blowing it to smithereens. If you saved less than five minutes ago or if rebuilding would take more time than re-doing what you've been doing, you might want to reload.

- Take the opportunity to make it better. We all get distracted by new projects and tend to leave old ones sitting for a long time. It's super common to jump in someone's world and see that their bedroom is a lot shabbier than whatever the newest project they're workin' on is, as miners often get so caught up in other stuff that they don't take the time to update or upgrade their older work. If a Creeper knocks a hole in your house, well maybe it's time to add that moat you've always wanted! This is one of the greatest things about Minecraft: when things get destroyed, it gives you the chance to make them better!

5. YOU FELL IN A PIT/CAVE/RAVINE WITHOUT TORCHES.

Falling into darkness is hard and a bit nerve-wracking; it usually starts with a bit of panic as you wonder how you can possibly get out without light. But...

- Just dig forward and up. Hopefully you have tools, but either way, just put a block in front of you (you can always kinda just a bit, even in the dark) and break it. Then point up and break the one above it, and then the one behind that. Jump up and repeat. You will eventually either A) find light, B) get out or C) crack into another drop and fall more, possibly to your death. Whatever happens, you'll at least get out.

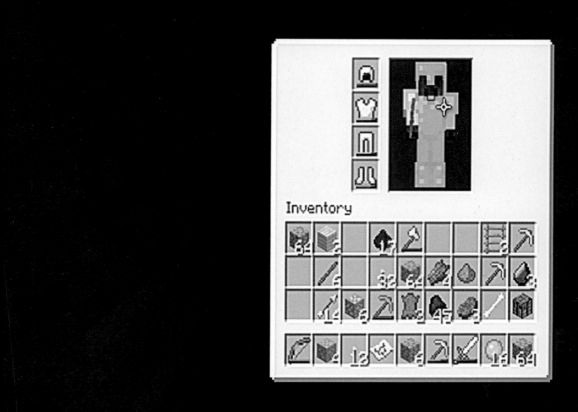

6. YOU HAVE A BUNCH OF RESOURCES AND WONDER IF IT'S TIME TO GO BACK, BUT AREN'T SURE IF YOU WANT TO YET.

Oh the many, many times we've thought to ourselves "I should find a Chest, but I'll just explore this one more cave." There's an answer:

- Don't stay out. If you're wondering if you should head to a Chest, the answer is almost always yes. Think of it like this: you just did a bunch of work, you have some good stuff, and you are currently safe, healthy and you know the way back. These are things you know for sure, right now. Give Minecraft the chance, and it will change one or all of those things within seconds. Err on the side of caution (and keeping your loot).

- Or, build a chest here and now and drop yer goods. You can always come back in a few minutes and grab it all, and at least you know it'll be safe.

- Or, save the game. Don't be afraid to use the save feature to your advantage. Hit pause and save real quick, that way you can load from right there and make a better decision if things go south.

7. YOU FIND SOMETHIN' AWESOME, BUT YOU AREN'T GEARED/PREPARED/READY TO JUMP INTO IT.

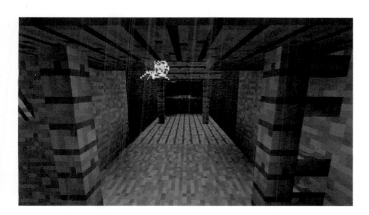

Abandoned Mineshafts are one of the more dangerous structures in the game. Don't go in unless you're ready.

Cool things are around almost every corner, and you'll end up stumbling across a ton of them while you were on your way elsewhere.

- Don't overreach. Taking a peek is fine, but if you don't think you're prepped for a big cave encounter, don't go down the big, dark, dangerous cave.

- Mark it well. Light the place up with Torches, build a big tower of Dirt, make a Flower path back home or better yet bust out a Map and write down the coordinates. Just because you aren't ready to go now doesn't mean you should let neat places and valuable areas be forgotten. Make it so you'll definitely be able to find it again, and then do.

8. A STRUCTURE OR AREA IS GIVING YOU TROUBLE BECAUSE IT IS GETTING TOO COMPLEX AND DANGEROUS.

In most games, you're pretty much stuck with having to navigate complex areas as they are, but this is Minecraft. We have better ways of dealing with nests of enemies, such as...

- Take the area apart. Just start simplifying the area by removing blocks and making it into one big room. You don't have to play fair; mobs certainly don't. Turn that confusing cave system or dangerous mineshaft into your area. Eliminate the threat by controlling the land, and you'll find that Fortresses and the like are just oh so much less intimidating.

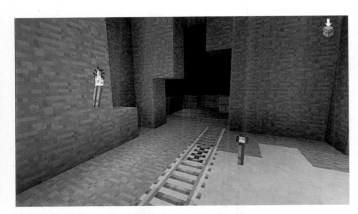

9. SOMETHING INTERESTING POPS UP WHILE YOU'RE IN THE MIDDLE OF A PROJECT.

Say you're carving out a base, and you stumble across the entrance to a cave or a big deposit of ore. What do you do? Abandon your project and deal with this now, or save it for later?

- If it's ore, go for it. Get ore until there is no more, and then fill in the area so it is just Cobblestone. Your later projects will thank you, and you won't lose the organization of what you were working on.

- If it's a structure or system, secure the area, mark it, and come back later. There is nothing more dangerous than leaving an entrance to an open cave or structure in your base or project, because you never know what can come sneaking up out of the depths all the way through your home and even to your bedroom. Where there's dark, there's danger. Control the situation first, finish what you were working on, then come back and dominate that structure and whatever foolish mobs dare to dwell in it.

10. YOU CAN'T FIND WHAT YOU'RE LOOKING FOR.

Sometimes you start a game and crack straight into a Diamond-filled ravine/Fortress, and sometimes you go weeks on a world without seeing either. While it's never guaranteed to find anything in the game, there is a system that can help.

- Use the Staircase Down, Ladder Up method. Seriously guys, this method works wonders. All you do is create a staircase down to the Bedrock and when you're at the bottom, build a Ladder that goes all the way to the surface from there. Create a few of these in different directions and on different parts of the map, and you end up covering an enormous area in very efficient manner. You'll find ore, you'll find structures, you'll find mobs; you'll find just about everything. Even more effective when combined with tunnels, branch mining and clearing out levels around the staircase.

GUIDE TO MINI-GAMES & ONLINE PLAY

Since even the earliest days of Minecraft, creative folks out there have been taking the rules of this blocky building game and have made entirely new games out of it! The many, many kinds of mini-games people have come up with inside of Minecraft is frankly amazing, and in fact some of them are so much fun that many players now do nothing but play them instead of the regular game!

This has especially become the norm for online Minecraft servers on the PC edition of the game, where mini-game playing has become an entire culture of its own. For those of you with the PC version, or those console or mobile players who are curious what kind of crazy things people have gotten up to with this game, here are 10 enormously popular Minecraft mini-games that change up the entire way you play the game, all in ways we love and think you will too.

Above: The great and mighty Walls, before they're brought crashing down. Note the pit beneath the wall of Sand, where it disappears into. Bottom: A group of players on a server prepare to enter The Walls.

THE WALLS

One of the very most popular and commonly found mini-games, The Walls was made by the legendary Hypixel (check out their entry in our Heroes chapter), and it's essentially basic PvP with a twist.

You and 3 other players or teams are dropped into one quadrant of a regular Minecraft world that has limits (meaning it's only so big). There are giant sand walls dividing your quadrant of the map from the other players, and a huge timer floating above everything. You have the time until the timer reaches 0:00 to prepare yourself and your area for battle, and once the timer does hit zero, the walls fall down!

At that point, it's an all-out brawl to see who can live the longest, and whoever does wins!

Note: you're not allowed to leave the designated map area, nor are you allowed to build over the height of the walls or knock down any of the wall on your own. Doing so will get you disqualified, so stick to the rules and have fun!

SKYBLOCK

Skyblock is one of the more challenging ways to play Minecraft, and it is so much fun. Not only that, but it'll actually help you learn quite a lot more about the game and its rules, and it can help give you ideas for regular play that you might not have had otherwise.

Skyblock involves you (or you and teammates) spawning on an island floating in the sky that is made of very few blocks. Usually it has a little Dirt, a tree (or just Saplings) and some Water and a Chest with a few items in it. What's in the Chest and what's on the island differ with various versions of the map (of which there are many), but the goal is almost always one of two things. One- you complete various tasks by creatively and efficiently using the items and blocks at your disposal, such as create 20 Cobblestone or gather 6 Wool, while staying alive (usually you only have one to three lives). Or two- in competitive Skyblock, you want to kill the other players, who have their own Skyblocks nearby, and be the last player or team standing.

Skyblock is intensely challenging because you have to be pretty knowledgeable about the rules of Minecraft in order to turn the few blocks and resources at your disposal into more things. For instance, if you do not start with any Cobblestone, you need to know how to make a Cobblestone generator out of Lava and Water. Or, in another example, you may need to build out a platform away from your island in order to let mobs spawn on it.

As we mentioned, there are *many* variations on this game, and you may find one server's version to be very different from another's. We'd suggest downloading either the SwipeShotTeam's Skyblock Warriors map (bit.ly/skyblockwarriorsmap) for an easy intro or, for those looking for a true challenge (and an intro into a bunch of great mods!), the incredible Agrarian Skies (downloadable through Feed the Beast mod loader found here: www.feed-the-beast.com).

Online Skyblock games often have starting areas such as this, where you choose your team.

A typical set of Skyblocks in a competitive server, before the mayhem begins.

A Skyblock can end up looking like this awesome island by britishcommando2 after a long period of hard work and dedication.

PARKOUR

Parkour is probably the easiest mini-game to learn the rules of, but one of the very hardest to master. All you're trying to do in Parkour is to jump from block to block on a pre-made course while not falling. If you fall, the courses are set up so that you have to start all the way over at the beginning, and if you make it to the end, you win!

Parkour courses can be anything from an actual mini-game set up with its own fancy map and server, maybe even with some Redstone scoring or other mechanisms set up, or it can just be a few blocks set up in a course on part of a map. Because it's so easy to set up, you'll find Parkour *everywhere* on servers, with many servers even building little Parkour courses across their spawn hubs or in mini-game waiting rooms.

Being good at Parkour is a bit of a badge of honor among Minecraft players online, and just about everyone gives it a shot. However, being that accurate with jumps is much harder than it looks, though with a little practice you'll find yourself getting better and better.

SPLEEF

The original big-time mini-game; the one that started the trend of making mini-games! Spleef isn't quite as popular on some big servers as it once was, but this is the mini-game that many of us think of as the official Minecraft mini-game, and it's still just as fun to play as it ever was.

Spleef is wild, and it's really not that hard to set up if you have a friend or two.

The concept is all about the set up, and it's pretty simple: a one-block-thick layer of Wool sits above a pool of Lava in an arena constructed of tough materials (such as Obsidian). Players start on top of the layer of Wool in the corners of the arena and use Flint and Tinder or Fire Charges to light the Wool on fire in the path of the other players. When the Wool burns, it disappears, leaving gaps in the floor through which players can fall. The last player who has stayed out of the Lava wins!

There are endless awesome variants on this game, such as including permanent blocks to jump to for safety, incorporating a maze into the arena, adding Ender Pearls to the mix (to teleport around the playing field), using multiple layers of Wool, throwing Eggs (Splegg!) or shooting Bows instead of lighting blocks on fire, or even putting blocks of TNT here and there to mix things up a bit.

Spleef arenas have become so popular that they're pretty much a genre of structure in Minecraft, and you can find Spleef maps on some servers or on PlanetMinecraft.com to download. Or, you can make your own version!

Above: Players in a server match of Survival Games wait for the clock to countdown so they can rush to the weapon chests in the center of the map. Bottom: MinecraftSurvivalGames.net has some of the best Survival Games maps out there, such as this one that is quite reminiscent of the film that the mini-game is based on.

SURVIVAL GAMES

Perhaps the most popular game people have created within Minecraft, Survival Games involves special maps that have been created for combat. It's based on a popular book/movie with a similar name, and the idea is that a group of players start the game near a bunch of chests filled with various items. At a signal, all players rush the items and try to grab as many as they can without getting killed, while also attacking other players.

Like said unnamed book/movie, when you die, you're out, and the last player standing wins. There are *tons* of these maps downloadable online, and many servers that host them, but you can also try making

your own! When playing online, make sure you read through the rules, as the type of items available and the things you can and can't do sometimes vary depending on the server.

PAINTBALL

Paintball is quick, easy and doesn't require much knowledge of the ins and outs of Minecraft.

Top and Middle: Flying Snowballs are a common sight in Paintball; in fact you'll probably never see so many in the air at once anywhere else in Minecraft! Bottom: Each match of Paintball has players select a team by picking a colored Wool block in a little pre-game room.

Paintball is pretty easy to pick up: all you do is run around a map trying to hit players with "paintballs," which are actually just Snowballs under a different name. If you hit a player once, they are immediately warped back to spawn and you and your team get points. The first team to get a certain amount of points or the team with the most points after a set amount of time wins. On some servers getting "kills" earns you coins that you can use to purchase powerups for either you or your team, like a triple-shot or reducing the amount of deaths your team has.

And that's it! Pretty simple, no? Don't be fooled though; while picking up a game of Paintball is easy and you're probably going to get at least a few kills in every match you play, there are some players that have taken this little mini-game rather seriously indeed and can hit other players with ease from far across the map. With practice, though, you can become one of these skillshot aficionados and start to get your name in the Top 3 of the scoresheet with regularity.

TNT RUN

A game that seems easy, and is another simple one to understand, but which will put your jumping and navigational skills to the test like few others. TNT Run has been around for a long time, and it involves running around in an arena on a flat surface which will fall out underneath you as you go. That means that if you step on a block, you better move quick because soon that block will drop and you'll fall to the next layer below.

The idea is to keep moving around and create holes in the ground as you move that other players fall into. Since these players are creating more holes themselves, you'll need to keep on your toes and plan out where you run, deftly jumping any holes that you can't run around.

When you fall to the next layer, you'll do the same thing there, and the player that is able to keep from falling through the final layer of the arena and into the darkness below is the winner.

Some players get a little confused about TNT Run's name, as there are no explosions in this mini-game. The reason the game is named after the 'splodiest block in Minecraft is that there is a block of TNT under each block that makes up the layers of the arena. The game has been specially designed so that walking on the Sand or Gravel blocks that make up the floor of each layer causes the TNT to activate beneath the Sand or Gravel, causing the Sand or Gravel to fall, though without causing an explosion. Essentially it's just a trick to get the game to work, so no need to worry about getting blown up in this mini-game. Just worry about where you're going to put your feet next!

Top and Middle: As you can see from these images, the maps in Wizards get absolutely wrecked by the end of a match, which is a major part of the fun. Bottom: Select your Wizard class before each match, or you can let it assign you one automatically.

WIZARDS

Who doesn't want to be a wizard? We know we're into the idea of wrathfully slingin' the powers of magic at our foes, and that's why we love the Wizards mini-game. This one is a simple PVP "capture the command point" mode that has each player pick a team and a kit, and each kit is a different type of wizard with a variety of unique powers.

The powers and wizard-types run the gamut from fireball throwers to ice wizards and more, and each class typically has an exploding spell attack that has a special feature to it, like a fireball that burns enemies (a Fire Charge shot when a staff is used), and a special defensive power, like an instant teleport. Most powers take "mana," which in this case is the icons in your hunger bar, which are used up quickly but also regenerate very quickly. Once you've selected your wizard-type, it's locked in for the rest of the match, so make sure to try a few out and find one you're good with.

The red pad with the beam of light coming out of it is one of the command points in a Wizards match, which you need to go stand on in order to secure it for your team.

Here's the list of Wizards classes and their powers:

FIRE WIZARD
Attack Power: Launches a fireball
Defense Power: Instant teleportation

KINETIC WIZARD
Attack Power: High damage, short-range railgun
Defense Power: Gravity gun

ICE WIZARD
Attack Power: Freeze shot to slow enemies
Defense Power: Puts up a wall of Ice

WITHER WIZARD
Attack Power: Exploding extra-poisonous Wither skull shot
Defense Power: An extra row of "absorption hearts"

BLOOD WIZARD
Attack Power: Normal attack costs 2 hearts instead of mana
Defense Power: Has a Splash Potion that instantly regenerates health

The matches themselves are set in an arena that is decently sized and typically contains all destructible blocks, which makes Wizards somewhat unique to PVP matches, which often feature indestructible arenas. Wizards arenas are like this because the powers at the disposal of each wizard in the match are mighty forces of nature that tend to explode and cause area damage, and part of the fun of Wizards matches is that the explosions wreck the environment as the match goes along. And, since the gravity is much lower in Wizards matches, you can jump just about anywhere, making every block in the arena part of the battleground. By the time a winner is announced, the whole arena will be in glorious ruins.

The combat in Wizards is a little different from many such fast-paced PVP mini-games, as although your spells have spectacular effects and do damage in an area, each wizard is actually pretty tough to kill and will not go down without more than a couple direct hits. Additionally, you aren't just trying to kill your enemies, you're also trying to walk on two different command points so that you capture them for your team. If enemy players are on the command point, they will start capturing it for their team instead, and the more players from one team on the command point, the more likely it is to go to that team. Once it's been captured, the other team has to keep enemy players off of it to capture it back, otherwise it will keep going fully back to the team that last captured it.

Points rack up for a team based on the amount of time a command point has been owned by that team, and when one team reaches 2000 points, they win this mighty struggle of magic users.

Wizards is as chaotic as it gets, but its balance of excellent unique classes, destructible terrain, low gravity, heavily armored players and the PVP + command points structure makes for one of the best PVP experiences in the world of Minecraft.

Most servers have hubs with portals like these, which teleport you to the land of the mini-game you want to play (Factions, in this case).

Factions bases can get intense, such as this one seen by Brewmaster_Luthor.

Over time, a basic little Factions hut can transform into a mighty fort, like this one shot by Phantomgamer.

FACTIONS

Looking for a mini-game that's a bit more long-term? Here's a goodie: Factions is a game that takes a regular Minecraft map and adds in the ability to join factions that can claim 16x16 chunks of land for their own. This land can't be built on, destroyed or otherwise tampered with (with a few exceptions) by anyone who is not a member of the faction.

Each player has what is called "power," and you can claim as many chunks as you have power (so with 10 power you can claim up to 10 chunks). If you die, however, you lose a power. If your power number goes below the number of chunks you have claimed, you will lose control over one of your chunks. You can join with other players in factions, which allows your power to be added to theirs (a player with 8 power can join a player with 10 to get 18 total). However, if any player in the faction dies, it takes one power from the faction's total. That means that if a player in your faction is killed 10 times, and your faction had 18 total power, you would then have just 8 power left. If you've already claimed 10 chunks of land for your faction, you would lose control of 2!

The goal is to maintain and expand the land you control while also attacking other factions to reduce their power. You can use special commands to join factions, or ally with, go neutral or go hostile to other factions.

There's no real "winner" in Factions, as new people can usually join and create new factions all the time, but Factions is a whole lot of fun to play over time, as you'll become very attached to your base and group. Things will change on the server, big attacks will happen and get talked about, and all sorts of other drama and action can occur. It's a very, very cool way to play, and it's one of the easiest mini-games to find on big servers.

From the Mindcrack UHC Season 16, this al-star team consisted of superMCGamer, oldGanon and Minecraft developer Dinnerbone.

Just about any amount of people can join in an Ultra Hardcore game. Here we have the Mindcrack crew gathered before the start of a new season. Many famous names in there!

Though there's crafting and exploration at the early stages of Ultra Hardcore, in the end it's all about who's left alive.

ULTRA HARDCORE

Outside of Skyblock, our favorite mini-game is Ultra Hardcore. This is a game with a ton of variations, but the central idea is the same between all versions: you have just one life, and you can only heal yourself with special, hard-to-make items (usually just Golden Apples, though servers differ on which items they allow to heal).

The best UHC (as it's known) servers in our opinion are those that have a decently large map with a world border of some sort (such as a wall, Water, a fall to death or a mod that adds a border), very few ways to heal and multiple teams, each using their own voice chat channels to communicate with their members.

When the game starts, every team will be transported to a random spot on the game map, and then it's on! You have to both craft and build up your resources (especially weapons, armor and healing items) quickly, but also watch out for and attack/defend against enemy teams. Whichever team has players left when all players on all other teams are dead wins!

It's a delicate balance, and there are a ton of strategies and competing philosophies out there on what makes the most effective UHC player, which makes UHC one of the best and most fun ways to play Minecraft for advanced Crafters. On top of that, it's actually a whole lot of fun to watch! In fact, we can't recommend enough heading over to the MindCrack YouTube channels (such as bit.ly/GuudeYouTube) to check out the MindCrack UHC competitions. It might sound weird if you've never tried it, but watching seriously good gamers play in a to-the-death competition with such intense rules is actually pretty thrilling!

SERVERS: WORLDS WAITING FOR YOU ONLINE

As varied as one person's Minecraft world is from another, servers are even crazier. There are plain Survival and Creative servers, role playing servers, competition servers, Factions servers and infinite more variations, and servers can hold as few as 0 other people or as many as 10,000+! It's one of the best parts of Minecraft, and each of the servers in our list here is absolutely worth at least a little peeking around.

2B2T
Server Address: 2b2t.org

So...2b2t is crazy. It is a world where the idea is that anything goes, at all, and it is not supposed to be reset ever. Unfortunately, it was reset once recently, due to the need for an update, but this is actualLy kind of good because as 2b2t goes along, it gets outright wild. This server is realLy like no other, and in fact, it's like no other thing in gaming. Because people cheat wildly, grief relentlessly and absolutely wreck the area for thousands of blocks around the spawn, 2b2t's landscape turns into a nightmare wasteland which you will probably not survive. Be warned: 2b2t is not for the faint of heart or the sensitive. You will die, people will attack you and wreck/steal whatever you have, and you will very likely run into some offensive language and behavior here. That being said, it's an experience like no other and completely fun, if you're ready for what awaits you.

One of the best parts of big servers like Arkham network is that everything from the hub to the mini-game maps is professionally designed and looks amazing.

ARKHAM NETWORK
Server Address: mc.arkhamnetwork.org

The Arkham Network consistently comes up in best-of lists for Minecraft servers because it is one of the most well-oiled and fun competitive servers that exist today. You'll almost always find thousands of other players on the Arkham Network no matter when you log in, and it features a semi-rotating crop of the most popular styles of play and mini-games, adding more as they are invented. As Minecraft communities go, this is one of the strongest, and they take entertaining you with mini-games very seriously.

Few servers can boast either hubs as gorgeous as Hypixel's or mini-games as fun and creative.

HYPIXEL
Server Address: mc hypixel net

The great Hypixel's personally hosted server, hypixel. net is another quality competition/PvP server and one of the more frequented servers period online. Since it is run by one of the bigger personalities in the game, you'll often find "celeb" players here as well as a very well-updated list of mini-games and competitions. Plus, because of the quality of folks involved, everything in it runs very smoothly and looks incredible! In fact, many mini-games were actually created specifically for this server, like the Blitz game we profile in our Mini-Games chapter of this book. Hypixel's home is a benchmark server for other servers, in that it's where trends are born and server methods are perfected, so why not spend a little time at one of the web's best locations?

MINDCRACK
Server Address: us.playmindcrack.com

There are actually two MindCrack servers (at least): the private one played on by Guude and the other members of the famous MindCrack Network, which is the subject of many incredibly popular YouTube video series', and then the public MindCrack server, which is this one. While it's pretty hard to get an invitation to the private MindCrack server, the public server is an example of the highest quality server that a regular Minecrafter can get on. Not only can you tour the maps from old seasons of the MindCrack video series', literally stepping virtual foot where some of the best Crafters in the world once built, you can also play the mini-games created by this untouchably talented crew of builders and YouTubers. Many of the great Redstone engineer SethBling's mini-game creations are tested first on this server, such as the wild and explosive Missile Wars game he created with Cubehamster, and indeed most of the mini-games found here are not seen elsewhere. Along with 2b2t, Hypixel and WesterosCraft, the MindCrack server sits among online royalty when it comes to public servers.

Here you see the team select for the awesome Mineplex Arcade, and the image above is of one of the games featured in said Arcade. In this game every player looks like a Villager and is in a sea of real Villagers. You have to try and figure out who is real and kill them, and every so often everyone changes into their normal form for a few seconds. Super fun!

MINEPLEX
Server Address: us.mineplex.com

A top mini-game server, Mineplex typically is one of the very busiest servers, often with over 10,000 players online at a time. In fact, at the time of this writing it has a whopping 13,354 Minecrafters on it enjoying the entertainments it has to offer. Mineplex is professionally run, with server hosts that really pay attention to the desires of their virtual denizens and who are constantly adding new features, tweaking things to be better and throwing special events just to make things that much more fun. Maybe one of the best features on any server is Mineplex's Arcade, where they mix up a ton of fun mini-games that play one after the other, so you only have to load into a lobby once.

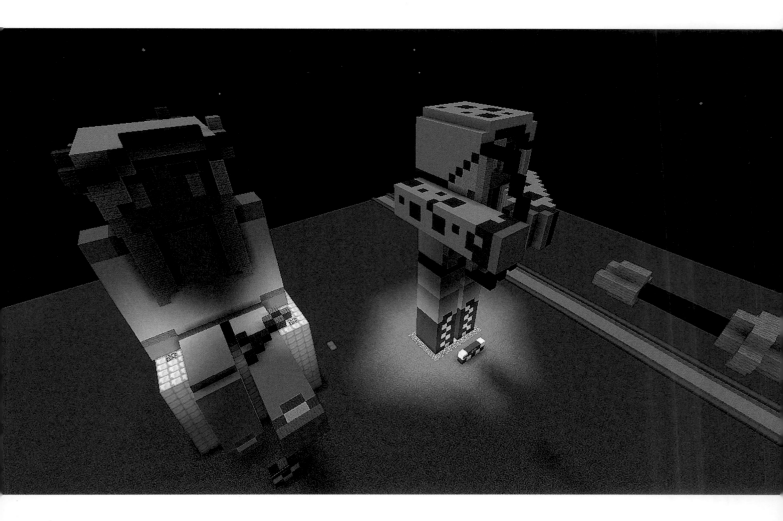

A personal favorite of this author, Lichcraft is a server that has just about every major mode and does all of it well.

LICHCRAFT
Server Address: us.lichcraft.com

Consistently ranked among the top (if not at the top) servers online, Lichcraft is similar to Hypixel and the Arkham Network but with a few different games to play, including Survival, Skygrid, kit PVP, Duels, Prison, MineZ and an excellent couple of Factions servers that are well populated and nicely run. It's just a solid server all around, and that's why it continues to be one of the best-known and most frequented servers in the game.

Treasure Island takes Creative Mode quite seriously, as is readily apparent when you spend a little time around the 0,0 coordinates, where most of the oldest and best plots are located.

TREASURE ISLAND
Server Address: ticreative org

Treasure Island is actually a collection of servers, like many of the others on this list, and it hosts many of the popular styles from PvP to Skyblock, but for here we're focusing on the subserver that focuses on Creative Mode. This is because the Treasure Island Creative server is incredible when it comes to the amount and quality of builds that can be found there. In fact, Treasure Island goes so far as to have a whole series of islands to build on and a system where players can judge other players' creations and give them points that earn ranks. The higher rank you are, the more islands you have access to build on, meaning that some islands are exclusively built on by those players that the community deems to be most skilled.

MCEdit < View Distance: 24 > Chunks: 1063 fps: 7.4 MBv: 308.9 cps: 0.7 Show Chunk View Record Undo ☑

Entities ☑
Items ☑
TileEntities ☑
TileTicks ☐
Unpopulated Chunks ☑
Chunks Borders ☐
Sky ☑
Fog ☑
Ceiling ☑
Chunk Redraw ☑
Hidden Ores ☐
Bedrock ☑
Coal ☑
Iron ☑
Lapis Lazuli ☑
Redstone ☑
Gold ☑
Diamond ☑
Nether Quartz ☑

Goto Dim

ck or drag to make a selection. Drag the selection walls to resize. Click near the ... :e wall.

SOFTWARE TO BOOST YOUR BUILDS

Here's a little secret about some of the amazing Minecraft builds and images you've seen: not all of them were actually made in normal Minecraft. GASP! Shocking right? It's a little weird to hear for the first time, but software outside of Minecraft itself is actually a pretty big part of the creation of many big or complicated Minecraft projects and screenshots.

Some folks are of a mind that Minecraft projects should be built by hand, block-by-block in the regular game, and that's totally fine, but there are others out there who see Minecraft as more of a creative medium than something that they want to toil at for weeks and weeks just to get a map done, and we think that's fine too.

When it comes down to it, we think it doesn't really matter how an awesome map gets made or a screenshot gets taken, it only matters that it's amazing and that we get to see it and/or play around

MCEdit will load up your Minecraft world in a couple of different views, including a map and one that looks pretty much like the game, but which can be flown around and edited with almost no lag (delay).

in it. Most of the time when you're in a map that used special software, you'll never know that it wasn't made the regular vanilla way, and in fact the ability to edit maps far more quickly and use special tools actually allows players to create types of maps that we would never see otherwise. For images, this is even more the case, as the programs that are out there to create Minecraft screenshots from a map are far, far more powerful and create much more gorgeous images than the game could ever create on its own.

If cutting down the amount of time it takes to create a building or making the most stunning screenshots possible is something that interests you, we definitely recommend checking out one of the following programs. And remember: you only have to use them as much or as little as you want, and the end result is what's most important, not the way you did it.

Oh, and all of these are totally free!

MCEdit
mcedit.net

What it is: A very powerful, yet pretty easy to use program that edits Minecraft worlds outside of the game

MCEdit is definitely the most widely-used Minecraft program besides the game itself, and many, many of the most popular maps were at least partly created using this bad boy. Essentially every block you need to place can be placed with MCEdit, but it also can do special things that you normally couldn't do, such as get a detailed map of your world quickly, place multi-block pieces down at once and use tools to "erode" the landscape in natural-looking patterns (which keeps you from having to try and do that manually, a tricky business).

The best parts about MCEdit are that your maps load and can be flown around very smoothly and with little system lag, and that it is crazy easy to use for being so powerful. Definitely worth your time for big projects.

VOXELSNIPER

dev.bukkit.org/bukkit-plugins/voxelsniper
kraftzone.net/wiki/VoxelSniper
thevoxelbox.com

What it is: An in-game editor and brush array that allows for editing a world at any distance and which features powerful terrain and object creation tools

Created by one of Minecraft's premier servers and builder communities, The Voxel Box, VoxelSniper is the in-game answer to MCEdit. Instead of loading your world up in software outside to edit, or having to build the regular way in-game, VoxelSniper allows you to add or remove blocks as far away as you can see in the game.

All you do is select the special "arrow" tool (to add) or the "gunpowder" tool (to delete), point at where you want to add or remove a block, and click, and it will do so!

Additionally, VoxelSniper comes with an array of "brushes" that will add or remove multiple blocks in specially designed patterns. You can set a brush size, then pick between brushes like the Erosion Brush, the Tree Brush, the Ring Brush and many many more, each of which places or removes blocks to create the effects that they're named after. The patterns these brushes make are very nicely designed and made specifically for Minecraft, so they end up having a great many uses in big creative worlds.

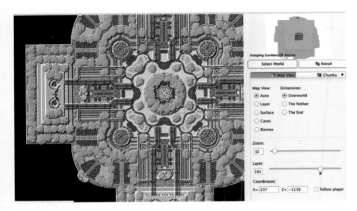

Renders in Chunky are set up by selecting portions of a build as seen from above (like it is here), and then adjusting the first person view.

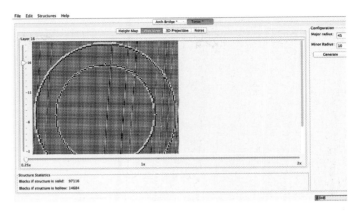

A view of Tectonicus, one of our Other Tools, which helps players to build certain shapes by giving them the design layer by layer.

CHUNKY

chunky.llbit.se

What it is: An outside of game tool that creates images of a world that are not possible to render in regular Minecraft

Compared to the last two tools, Chunky is quite a bit more complicated to use, partially because the language it uses and the concepts it deals with are more about image rendering and creation than about playing Minecraft. That being said, many of the very best Minecraft screenshots are created with Chunky, and those looking to show off what they've built will find it invaluable to their efforts.

Basically what it does is to load your world outside of Minecraft in an editor that shows you a visual map from the top down, allowing you to select the chunks of the map you would like in your image. You then create a "scene," which loads from the perspective of where your character was when you saved last, or you can place the view in a specific spot. You can then move the view around a little bit and tweak a wide array of settings to create exactly the image that you want before you render and save it.

You can get pretty insanely creative with this tool, even setting things like the height of the sun, the focus

of the camera, the exposure amount and more, and the images that result are often quite beautiful. They also, however, can take quite a while to both set up and to render, so it's not a tool for quick-shots, but instead for the ones you want to make perfect.

OTHER TOOLS

The tools we've listed here are just the most popular and powerful of many, many available tools. A few others to check out, if these ones piqued your interest, include:

- JourneyMap (mapping)
- Tectonicus (mapping)
- AMIDST (finds dungeons and villages)
- Minecraft X-Ray (can see through maps to find items and blocks)
- Minecraft Editor (map editor)
- Terrain Control (custom biome and land creation)
- MCDungeon (makes dungeons and "treasure hunts" in already created maps)
- NovaSkin (skin editor)
- MCSkinner (skin editor)
- Minecraft Texture Studio (create your own resource packs)
- INVedit (inventory editor)
- Mineways (export your world to a 3D printer)

Google   minecraft   🔍   ⠿ jason@intersectmedia.com ▾

Web   Videos   News   Images   Shopping   More ▾   Search tools   ⚙

About 130,000,000 results (0.17 seconds)

Minecraft
https://**minecraft**.net/ ▾ - Minecraft ▾
Minecraft is a game about breaking and placing blocks. At first, people built structures to protect against nocturnal monsters, but as the game grew players ...

Download it here
... the game, you can download the stand-alone launcher for ...

To Play The Demo
Minecraft. Please log in or register for a Mojang account to play ...

Log in
Minecraft is a game about placing blocks to build anything you ...

Store
Minecraft is a game about placing blocks to build anything you can ...

More results from minecraft.net »

In the news

Play Info Quest II. You might learn something...
Mojang - 2 days ago
... on this entry are closed. Previous post: **Minecraft** 1.8.2-pre1 -- Christmas Gift Edition. Next post: **Minecraft** Skin Studio Encore now available!

Minecraft Creator's New $70m Beverly Hills Mansion, Rebuilt in Minecraft
GameSpot - 6 hours ago
Of Course Someone Made Notch's $70 Million Mansion In Minecraft
Kotaku - 1 day ago

More news for minecraft

Minecraft - Wikipedia, the free encyclopedia
en.wikipedia.org/wiki/**Minecraft** ▾ - Wikipedia ▾
Minecraft is a sandbox independent video game originally created by Swedish programmer Markus "Notch" Persson and later developed and published by the ...

Official Minecraft Wiki - The ultimate resource for all things ...
minecraft.gamepedia.com/ ▾
Welcome to the **Minecraft** Wiki, a publicly accessible and editable wiki for information related to **Minecraft**. The wiki and its 3,620 articles and 10,213 files are ...

Minecraft
Video game

★★★★★ 4.5/5 - Google Play
★★★★★ 4.5/5 - Apple

Minecraft is a sandbox independent video game originally created by Swedish programmer Markus "Notch" Persson and later developed and published by the Swedish company Mojang since 2009. Wikipedia

Initial release date: May 17, 2009

Developers: 4J Studios, Mojang

Designers: Jens Bergensten, Markus Persson

Awards: VGX Award for Best Independent Game, BAFTA Games Special Award

Platforms: Android, PlayStation 3, PlayStation Vita, PlayStation 4, More

Publishers: Sony Computer Entertainment, Microsoft Studios, Mojang

People also search for   View 5+ more

Terraria   Grand Theft   Garry's Mod   World of   Counter-...
2011   Auto V   2004   Warcraft   1999
                2013   2004

Feedback

MINECRAFT ON THE WEB:
Sites To Enhance Your Game

If you thought Minecraft's domination of your computation machine ended at the game itself, get ready to be awed at the ever-widening scope of this deceptively humble game. Minecraft has a massive online presence, with so very many websites dedicated to various aspects of the game that it feels like they're just about infinite.

Among those thousands and thousands and, yes, more thousands of sites are a few that have become an integral part of many players' Minecraft experience. Knowing which of these sites to go to and what they're good for can not only improve your skills at the game, it can also provide all new experiences. From watching the Let's Plays of YouTube where Minecraft celebrities film their exploits, to downloading the latest greatest maps off of Planet Minecraft to chatting with fellow Crafters on the Forum and Reddit, it's a big, wide world of Minecraft out there on the Internet, and it's waiting for you just a few clicks away.

Here we'll introduce you to the best of the best of these many sundry sites to get you started on your WebCraft explorations.

PLANET MINECRAFT

planetminecraft.com

Focus: Downloading, showcasing and uploading maps, skins, texture packs and servers, plus a large forum

Planet Minecraft is by far the most important website to the Minecraft creator community. Though there are other sites (especially those of individual creators) where you can download maps, skins and texture packs to play with in your own Minecraft game, Planet Minecraft is far and away the biggest, best and most popular repository of everything downloadable for Minecraft.

Nearly all the big names are on here, from SethBling to disco to Circleight to carloooo and more, and pretty much every famous map or game type or construction type can be found in the databases of Planet Minecraft. Heck, most of the maps we feature in our books were found on PM!

Not only can you download projects here, you can interact with the people who do, commenting on their maps and giving "Diamonds" to vote on the best projects, and you can even upload your own works for free! Got something you want to show off? Put it up on Planet Minecraft, and if it's good, it's almost guaranteed to be seen by thousands of people.

PM is amazing, and with literally thousands of new projects up every month, it's a never-ending parade of new things to try out. Mini-games, adventure maps, Redstone tutorials, PVP arenas, massive, amazing worlds to explore-it's all here!

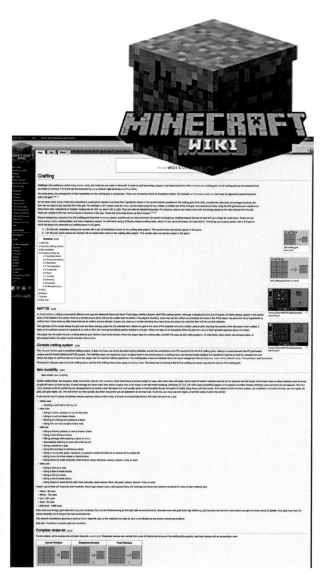

A typical Minecraft Wiki page, this one detailing the basics of crafting in the game. Pages on the Wiki range from the very short (stubs on some items, for instance), and the quite long, such as this entry or the one on Redstone.

THE MINECRAFT WIKI
minecraft.gamepedia.com

Focus: Information on many aspects of the game

Where Planet Minecraft is all about adding to your game, the Minecraft Wiki is there to give you information that you need to play. While it can be disorganized and some entries aren't kept up to date or written as well as others, if you need to know something quickly about an item or a specific aspect of the game, the Minecraft Wiki is where you want to go. It has a pretty straightforward search feature that will quickly bring you to the page on, as an example, potions, giving you all of the recipes and a bit about the concepts behind the subject. There's a ton of info here, though it's pretty self-guided and can vary in quality from entry to entry.

What definitely is awesome about the Wiki, however, is that it keeps a detailed history of Minecraft, from the content of each update to information on the history of its creation. That stuff is pure gold if you're into Minecraft trivia, and it can be a lot of fun to explore the thousands of pages and become even more of a Minecraft expert.

If you feel up to the task and have a little free time, you can actually become a contributor to the Minecraft Wiki by making an account and going through a vetting process. Contributors have to prove themselves, but eventually you can put your Minecraft knowledge to use tackling the ever-growing, never finished pile of "Wanted Articles" and "Stubs" that the Wiki would like to see added. It's a pretty cool way to be a part of the Minecraft community, and the top contributors are highly respected among older Crafters. You'll get to be a part of important conversations about the game, and even see some of the Mojang guys on there sometimes!

Page | Talk | Share ▾ | View | View source | History

Search

MINECRAFT WIKI

- 🌐 Community portal
- 🗂 Admin noticeboard
- 🏳 Wiki rules
- ⤢ Create an account
- ⤢ Help contents
- 🗺 How to help
- 🔖 Style guide
- 🔖 Copyrights
- ▽ General disclaimer

Recent changes · New pages · Missing pages

Welcome to the Minecraft Wiki, a publicly accessible and editable wiki for information related to *Minecraft*. The wiki and its 3,617 articles and 10,214 files are managed and maintained by 340 active contributors from the *Minecraft* community, along with the wiki's administration team. Anyone can contribute.

Navigation sidebar:

Main page
Community portal
Projects
Wiki rules
Recent changes
Admin noticeboard
Directors page

▾ Minecraft
  Website
  Forums
  Mojang blog
  Issue tracker
  Facebook page
  YouTube channel
  Steam community
  Minecraft Museum
  Server list
  Classic server list
  IRC

▸ Useful pages
▸ Gamepedia
▸ Tools

▾ In other languages
  Deutsch
  Español
  Français
  Magyar
  Italiano
  日本語
  한국어
  Nederlands
  Polski
  Português do Brasil
  Русский
  中文

VAINGLORY WIKI

About *Minecraft*

MINECRAFT is a sandbox construction game created by Mojang AB founder Markus Persson, and inspired by the *Infiniminer*, *Dwarf Fortress* and *Dungeon Keeper* games. Gameplay involves players interacting with the game world by placing and breaking various types of blocks in a three-dimensional environment. In this environment, players can build creative structures, creations, and artwork on multiplayer servers and singleplayer worlds across multiple game modes.

Minecraft is available to all players for €19.95 (US$26.95, £17.95). When purchased, singleplayer and multiplayer game modes can be played using the downloadable stand-alone launcher. *Minecraft* Classic is available to play for free. *Minecraft* development started around May 10, 2009, and pre-orders for the full game started being accepted on June 13, 2009. *Minecraft's* official release date was November 18, 2011. On September 20, 2014, *Minecraft* for the computer reached 17 million sales and became the best-selling PC game of all time.

On August 16, 2011, *Minecraft: Pocket Edition* was released for the Sony Xperia Play gaming smartphone. After its exclusivity with Sony expired, it was released for Android devices on October 7, 2011, and iOS devices on November 17, 2011 for US$6.99. On April 2, 2014 *Minecraft* was released for the Amazon Fire TV. It contains all the same features as the *Pocket Edition* as well as support for the Fire TV's controller.

On May 9, 2012, *Minecraft* was released for the Xbox 360 on Xbox Live Arcade for US$20, where it subsequently broke every previous sales record.

On February 11, 2013, *Minecraft: Pi Edition* was released for the Raspberry Pi. It is based on the *Pocket Edition* and is available for free at Mojang's dedicated blog. The *Pi Edition* is intended as an educational tool for novice programmers and users are encouraged to open and change the game's code using its API.

On December 17, 2013, *Minecraft* was released for the PlayStation 3 on the PlayStation Store for US$19.99. The release was almost identical to the Xbox 360 Edition and was developed in tandem with the Xbox 360 Edition from then on.

On June 26, 2014, the Xbox 360 & PlayStation 3 editions' sales passed the number of sales for the PC edition of *Minecraft*, leaving the *Minecraft* series having sold more than 54 million copies world-wide and become third best-selling video game of all time.

Minecraft was released for the PlayStation 4 on September 4, 2014, the Xbox One on September 5, 2014 and the PlayStation Vita on October 14, 2014.

On September 15, 2014, Mojang AB and all of its assets (including *Minecraft*) were purchased by Microsoft for US$2.5 billion.

On December 10, 2014, *Minecraft: Pocket Edition* was released for Windows Phone 8.1.

Play it!

Computer edition

Game 1.8.1 Launcher 1.5.3

Pocket Edition

Android	iOS	fireTV	Windows
0.10.4	0.10.4	0.10.0	0.10.4

Console Edition | **Pi Edition**

Xbox 360	Xbox One	PS3	Raspberry Pi
TU16	TU1	1.06	0.1.1

PS4	PSVITA
1.01	1.01

Purchase the computer edition! (Demo)
Purchase the Pocket Edition! Android · iOS · Amazon Fire TV · Windows Phone 8.1
Purchase the Console Edition! Xbox 360 (Demo) · Xbox One · PlayStation 3 (Demo) · PlayStation 4 (Demo) · PlayStation Vita (Demo)
Download the Raspberry Pi Edition!

Gameplay

Explanation of the various game modes and features used in *Minecraft*.

Game modes
- Survival
- Creative
- Hardcore
- Adventure
- Spectator
- Demo

Recipes
- Crafting
- Smelting
- Brewing

Tutorials
- New player
- General
- Mining
- Item farming
- Mob farming
- Enchanting & smelting
- Mechanism
- Technical

Popular and useful pages

Achievements
Information on achievements that can be collected in *Minecraft*.

Blocks
Detailed information on the various blocks available in *Minecraft*.

Items
Detailed information on the various items available in *Minecraft*.

Biomes
Information about all biomes in *Minecraft*.

Enchanting
Information about enchanting.

Mobs
Information about the various friendly and non-friendly creatures found in *Minecraft*.

Trading
Detailed information about villager trading.

Redstone circuits
Information about redstone circuits.

Resource packs
Various resource packs that alter the look and feel of the game.

Modifications
Various modifications that alter the gameplay.

News and events

News

October 14, 2014
Minecraft: PlayStation Vita Edition was released.

September 15, 2014
Minecraft and Mojang were bought by Microsoft.

September 5, 2014
Minecraft: Xbox One Edition was released.

September 4, 2014
Minecraft: PlayStation 4 Edition was released.

August 1, 2014
Minecraft End-User License Agreement started to be enforced on all servers.

Recent updates

November 24, 2014
Minecraft 1.8.1 released.

November 18, 2014
Minecraft Alpha 0.10.0 released for the Pocket Edition.

September 2, 2014
Minecraft 1.8 released.

July 10, 2014
Minecraft Alpha 0.9.0 released for the Pocket Edition.

June 26, 2014
Minecraft 1.7.10 released.

Note the similarities between the Minecraft Wiki and Wikipedia–if you know how
to use Wikipedia, you should be comfortable navigating this page as well.

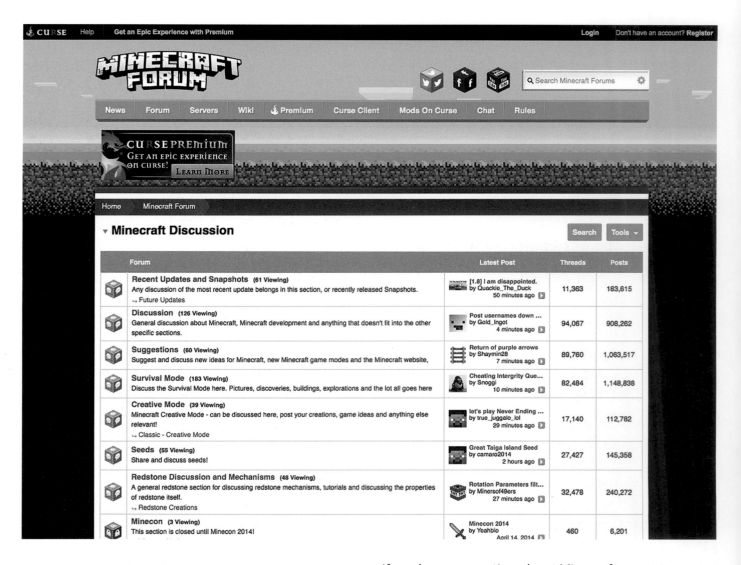

MINECRAFT FORUM

minecraftforum.net

Focus: Talking with others about all aspects of the game, as well as finding new maps, mods and more

The number one website for Crafters to gather and talk about Minecraft is the Minecraft Forum. Here anyone can make an account and chat with other Minecrafters about whatever they like, whether that's finding a new server, showing off screenshots, talking strategy or even chatting about other things that aren't Minecraft.

If you have a question about Minecraft, want to show something off that you did or want to find a new server to play on or new people to play with, the Minecraft Forum should be your first stop. Chances are, whatever your question or need, someone else has either asked the same question or can help you out quickly.

It's also common practice for most big mods, shaders, servers and some maps to have a page on here where their creators post information and the latest downloads for their creations. While Planet Minecraft has a lot of this stuff, the Forum usually has the most up-to-date version and a lot more info, and you'll find yourself going back and forth between the two sites a lot if you get into downloading add-ons for your game.

One thing to note about the forums: while they are heavily moderated, anyone can get on here, so be careful with what you post and who you talk to if you're still a young Crafter. Of course, most people on the Forum are super nice and happy to help you get better at the game, so don't worry too much, just keep your eye out for bad eggs.

And always remember: be nice and don't spam!

YOUTUBE
youtube.com

Focus: Let's Play videos of Minecrafters recording their gameplay, lists of great mods and maps, and tutorials for most things you'd want to try

The three previously mentioned sites are the biggest and best out there when it comes to Minecraft-specific content, but YouTube may be the most important Minecraft site when it comes to spreading and teaching the game. This is because in recent years gamers have taken to recording themselves playing games, especially Minecraft, and have uploaded videos of themselves doing so to the site.

Nowadays, it's one of the most popular topics on YouTube, and many folks have actually become Minecraft celebrities that make a living posting hilarious, insightful and downright entertaining Minecraft videos on the website.

Some of the biggest names include the Mindcrack group (Guude, SethBling, Nebris et al.), SkyDoesMinecraft, CaptainSparklez, stampylonghead, SSundee, TheDiamondMinecart and the ever popular Yogscast. Many of these folks have been on here a very long time and have millions of subscribers, not to mention videos that can rack up hundreds

Even your trusty author has his own YouTube channel under the name DEFENDERPLAYSGAMES (note, channel meant for mature audiences).

of thousands or even millions of views each. They typically are very entertaining, having refined their, *ahem*, Craft for years and over thousands of videos, and each one has a massive following that they interact with regularly. If you've never seen a Minecraft Let's Play, we suggest checking out Mindcrack's UHC videos, one of Yogscasts series' or one of the many, many Minecraft music videos out there to start off.

In addition to the entertainment value, YouTube is ideal for showing players how various things work in the game. Can't figure out how to make a Redstone gate, or curious what a certain mod does? Search for it on YouTube! We can absolutely guarantee someone has explained it very well on there, if not many someones.

If you like the idea of using YouTube for Minecraft, you can actually join yourself and start uploading your very own videos! You'll need some special software and a microphone, but it's pretty simple to do when you get it set up. And, not surprisingly, you can find out how to do all that set up on YouTube itself.

MODLOADER SITES

files.minecraftforge.net
feed-the-beast.com
technicpack.net

Focus: Getting you those sweet, sweet mods and keeping you up to date with the modding community

Most major mods for Minecraft have a specific forum page dedicated to them, as mentioned, but the primary way most mods are announced and accessed is through a modloader page.

Forge is more about getting the actual loader itself, which is slightly complex, but the site contains good and easy walkthroughs to get you through it.

Feed the Beast and Technic, on the other hand, are pretty slick and actually have the mods accessible through the loaders themselves, meaning you don't have to do much except get the modloader downloaded from the website. Those last two especially are great for learning about new mods and reading the information about them, as they will give pretty detailed accounts and post fairly often (Technic most of all, perhaps).

There are other mod sites out there as well, so do a little exploring and see if you find one you really like!

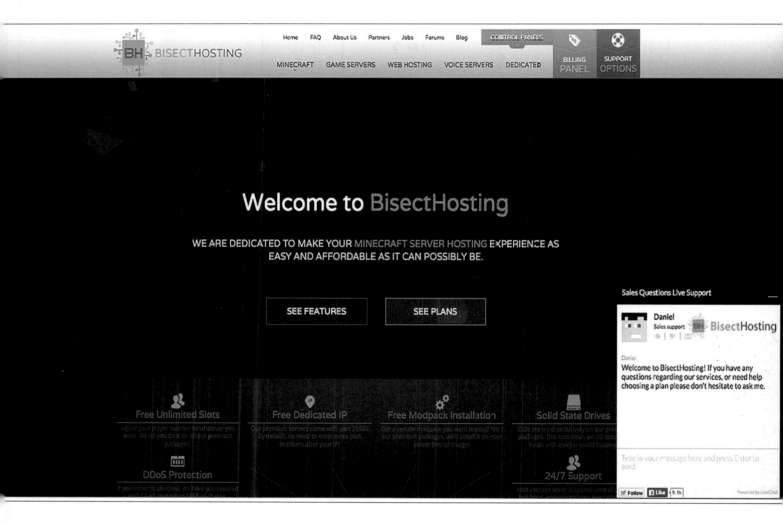

SERVER HOSTING SITES
Many, many out there!

Focus: Sites that you can pay to host a private or public Minecraft server

If you play Minecraft on the PC, chances are you've thought about how cool it would be to be able to play with your friends on your own server. While you can always play a LAN game with friends, or get on a public server, if you want to play on a private world with people online, you either have to have your own dedicated server running or know someone who does.

Setting up a server is totally do-able, but it takes a lot of time and effort, and a lot can go wrong. Try and add something like mods or big maps in there, and you'll quickly run into trouble. Typically people need an entire computer dedicated to running the server, plus a lot of expertise on server upkeep.

That's where server hosting sites come in: you just pay them a monthly fee, and they do the work and set up a server for you. There are a ton of options out there when it comes to pricing and what you get for your dollar, including hosts that will add mods for you, servers that allow many people to join at once and much more.

It's not something all players will want to do, but there really is something special about getting your own permanent game going with friends from all over the world, so if that sounds fun, definitely check out server hosting sites online.

SKINS, RESOURCE PACKS AND SHADERS:
Making Your Minecraft Pretty

Minecraft is rather unique among games- this is something all players know. One way that it is unique that can sometimes go overlooked, however, is that Minecraft's structure of being mostly blocks with textures on them allows the look of Minecraft to be customized to a degree that few other games have ever seen. Because players and creative folk out in the world can basically take that blocky structure and create their own textures to lay over it, the exact same world and characters can be changed in nearly infinite ways to look differently, making for perhaps the most customizable visuals in any game ever created.

There are three basic components to Minecraft's visuals that can be customized: skins, texture or "resource" packs, and the trickier, but oh so awesome shaders. If you're looking to pretty up your Minecraft game and create an entirely unique look that can sometimes change even a standard Minecraft landscape into something worthy of a million screenshots, here's how you do that.

SKINS:
Changing Your Character's Look

By far the easiest facet of your Minecraft visuals to give a facelift to is literally the face (and body) of your Minecraft character. Ole Steve, your standard Minecraft character model, is great and all, but at some point when playing online it gets pretty boring to look like every other schmoe out there. That's when it's time to change your Minecraft skin, and doing so is very, very easy.

How to Change
PC/Mac- Changing your skin on the PC or Mac versions of the games is actually done online through the official Minecraft website. Just head over to minecraft.net and click on the "Profile" button at the top of the screen. Sign into your profile, and the very next page will ask you if you want to change your skin. All you do then is to select one of the two character models (the only difference is that one has slightly skinnier arms), and then you click "Browse" and find the skin file on your computer. After that it's just a matter of uploading the file! Super simple, all around.

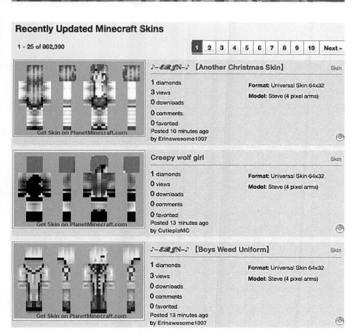

Console: Skins on console versions are changed in the game menu when you're in a game. Skins are located under the Help & Options menu, and though you can't upload custom or self-made skins like you can for PC or Mac, there are many, many skinpacks available on console to purchase, most of which have a free trial with a few free skins in them.

Where to Get Skins

Kind of a creepy sentence, no? Well, in this case, we're talkin' the non-fleshy kind of skins, so don't worry. Skins for the PC and Mac version are readily available online in the thousands, and finding them is as simple as heading to a skin database (another creepy phrase!) and just picking one out and downloading it.

A few of the biggest skin databases include Planet Minecraft, The Skindex, MinecraftSkins. net and the SkinCache.

Making Your Own Skin

The creepy sentences keep coming! Making your own skin is a pretty simple process, as all skins are actually just a flat image that is wrapped around the character model. A wide variety of programs exists out there to help you create and test skins yourself, and it does not take much time to become a master skinner. Some of the best include NovaSkin, Miners Need Cool Shoes and MCSkinner, the first two of which are actually used completely online in a browser. The Minecraft Wiki has a great list of skinning programs to check out if creating your own look interests you, so just Google "Minecraft skin program," and you'll see the list.

Top: The page on minecraft.net where skins can be changed for PC/Mac/Linux. Middle: A few minutes on any big Minecraft server will show you the wild variety of skins that are out there. Bottom: A typical selection of fan-made skins on PlanetMinecraft.

RESOURCE/TEXTURE PACKS

Where skins change the look of your character, resource packs, also called texture packs, change the look of the actual blocks in your game. They can also change things like the way Water looks and the way the sky and even the sun and moon appear, making them very powerful tools to create a new experience in your game.

How to Change

PC/Mac- Mojang has included a nice little shortcut in Minecraft to make adding a new resource pack quite easy. Simply start up the game, and then go to Options in the menus. Click on Resource Packs, and then hit the Open Resource Pack Folder button. You'll then need to either quit the game or turn Fullscreen to OFF in the Video settings, and you will see a window open that is the folder named Resource Packs. Then, simply copy-paste the .zip resource pack files that you want to add into the folder!

Top: Changing resource packs is simply a matter of navigating to the right menu after you instal them. Middle: Even the menus can look quite different when you load up a resource pack. Bottom: Minecraft almost looks like a totally new game with packs, so experiment and find one that makes your world look the best!

Console: Like skins, resource packs on the console are limited to the ones that are officially available, but there are quite a few of these out there. On the console, resource packs are officially known as "texture packs," and they must be loaded before you load the actual game world. It's actually one of the options when you select a world, right there on the screen as you confirm your selection, and you simply pick the one you want. Like skins, you can also purchase extra texture packs if you wish for pretty cheap ($1).

Where to Get Resource/Texture Packs

Resource/texture packs for the PC and Mac can also be found online, again at sites like Planet Minecraft, resourcepack.net, MinecraftTexturePacks.net and Curse's Minecraft Texture Packs page. The Minecraft Forum is perhaps the best place to get packs, as you'll see players upload them and update very frequently, and it provides a great place for other players to post pictures of their worlds with the packs turned on and discuss them.

Making Your Own Resource Packs

This is also totally possible, though it is much, much more intensive than creating a Minecraft skin. Again, there are a wide variety of programs out there to help you out with this, and using Google to find the Minecraft Wiki's Resource Pack Creators page is your best bet. Successfully creating a resource pack is a pretty big undertaking however, as you'll need to think carefully about how every texture you create will look in your world and together with the textures of other blocks. We'd suggest using YouTube to get some tutorials on the specific program you choose, which should help tremendously.

The same scene in a variety of shaders. Particularly note the differences in the Water, the shadows and the way the focus works.

SHADERS

Shaders are by far the most powerful visuals-changing feature of the game, as they actually change the way that light and pixels are displayed. When you've seen those really gorgeous photos of Minecraft with lots of realistic shadows and lighting effects, they are always created in a Minecraft world that has shaders enabled.

It's by far one of the most dramatic ways to change your game, with some players saying that they simply can't go back to playing without shaders on. However, shaders are PC/Mac/Linux only, they're somewhat difficult to install, and they require a pretty powerful computer to be able to run and actually play the game (and not just take a quick screenshot).

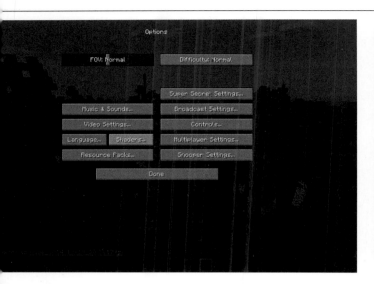 

How to Change

There are a few built-in shaders for Minecraft on the computer, which can be found by clicking the "Super Secret Settings" button in the menus in-game. However, these are mostly just pixel shaders and not very good to play with. The shaders that people use to actually play the game require that you install the Forge modloader (files and instructions at files. minecraftforge.net), and you then need to install the Shaders Mod (found at http://bit.ly/ShadersModLink with instructions).

Once this is installed, you'll need to make a shaderpacks folder in your main Minecraft folder (the same place where you find the folders for your screenshots, saves and mods), and then download and place shaderpacks into the shaderpacks folder. Once you've got it all set up like the instructions at the Shaders Mod page tell you, you'll be able to load your

Forge mod profile through the Minecraft launcher, open a world, and then hit the ESC key to go to your options. In your Video settings you will now have a Shaders option, where you can select which shader you want to use.

Where to Get Shaders

There aren't nearly as many shaders out there to download as skins and resource packs, but some of our favorites, and the ones used in this book, include Sonic Ether's Unbelievable Shaders, Sildur's Vibrant Shaders, MrMeep_x3's Shaders and DocteurDread's Shaders. Most of these have their own page on the Forums, so just Google the name and you'll find them easily.

REDSTONE BASICS

Ready to start your journey to becoming a master of all that is Redstone? Well then, let's dive right on in and get familiar with the basics of the Redstone world! Before we do so, however, lets talk for a moment about how to best use this chapter to get the most out of it and to become the most knowledgable Redstone engineer you can.

Redstone is a massive topic, almost infinitely so because there are always players finding new ways to use it, and also because it often gets updated when Minecraft itself gets an update.

This chapter is meant to give you all of the basic information you need to begin learning how to use Redstone in the easiest and most pain free way we can teach it to you. We want to make Redstone fun and inviting, and to dispel the air of intimidation and difficulty that often surrounds the subject.

That being said, these concepts are also very complex, and there's a lot of information to internalize, so we'd also make one more suggestion for how to have the best and most successful Redstone learning experience:

Don't worry about getting it all perfect. Even the best Redstone engineers out there took a long time to understand and memorize this information, and there's no rush to do so. The best way to learn Redstone is to read through this chapter and test out the different builds, and then to just keep messing around with the stuff, referring back to the book when you need to

know something. Over time, you'll start to naturally remember the nitty gritty details of Redstone items, rules and concepts without having to look them up, so there's no need to get discouraged if you keep having to look back at the book as you go.

In fact, we'd even suggest seeking out more resources on Redstone as well, such as watching videos online or finding other players to learn from. This chapter is meant to be your introduction to the world of Redstone and a handy reference guide, but we won't have our feelings hurt if you need to seek out a little extra help! The goal here is to help you learn Redstone, and we are simply trying give you as many resources in these pages as possible to help you do that.

One final note before we get going: Almost everything we talk about in this chapter assumes that you are playing in Creative Mode. This is because the builds take very, very many items of different types, and while you might have them in your Survival World, they will be pretty expensive. Additionally, Creative Mode allows you to fly and to turn off hostile mobs, allowing you to be able to learn in peace. We can't suggest doing this enough to learn Redstone's rules. Additionally, this book is primarily focused on the full version of Minecraft as it is on the PC and Mac. This is because the console versions do not contain all Redstone items quite yet, but they are being updated frequently. If you are playing on a console, you'll have to wait to try some of these concepts until the updates happen, but the basic rules and many of the builds are still the same and will work.

With that in mind, let's get into this!

THE CONCEPT

In a nutshell, Redstone is a system that uses power signals to cause something to happen in the game of Minecraft. This "something" could be as simple as opening a Door or turning on a light, or it could be something a bit more complex like causing a mechanism such as a Piston to activate and interact with the world, or it could be as complex as causing a mini-game to begin. A simple Redstone power signal can even cause something as intricate and massive as a player-built Redstone simulation of a computer to turn on and function!

Redstone power is somewhat like real-life electricity, and thinking of it like this is very useful, especially when first starting out with the stuff. Here are the ways in which Redstone and real-world electricity are similar:

- Redstone has an ON state and an OFF state.

- Redstone signals can have various levels of power, in the case of Redstone it goes from 0-15.

- Redstone signals can be carried through a Minecraft world through items called Redstone Dust (as well as others) that are very similar to real-life wires.

- A powered Redstone signal that is "wired" up so that it runs into certain items in the game called "mechanisms" will give those mechanisms power and cause them to activate.

- Redstone can be used to build "circuits" that function in much the same way as real-life circuits function in computers and other electronics.

There are, however, quite a few ways in which Redstone and normal electricity differ, and they are equally important:

The power that Redstone builds use is not always held in a storage unit like a battery, or piped through from the outside, but is instead almost always created by the items that toggle the power ON and OFF. To further explain the difference, a real-world light switch controls electric power, but it does not create the power. In Minecraft, Levers, which are very similar in look to light-switches, can control Redstone power, but they also create that power themselves. Redstone items that create power are called "power components," and there are many types of these, including two that do act somewhat like a battery and/or permanent power source (Redstone Torches and Blocks of Redstone).

Redstone power signals only go 15 blocks in one direction before their power signal fades away. To get it to go farther, it must be boosted. This is actually similar to real electricity, except that the rules that govern the distance of real electric signals are far more complex.

Redstone signals can and often are influenced by the passage of time. This is also actually similar to real electricity, but again there is a major difference. This time the difference is that the time delays on real electricity are often so fast that we do not even recognize them, while in Redstone this is essentially slowed way down so that players can manipulate and use these delays. Time in Redstone is measured in "ticks," where each a tick happens 10 times a second, or once every 0.1 seconds in real time. Redstone components and mechanisms update their status every tick, checking to see if their inputs have changed in any way, and when the input does change, they respond by activating, deactivating or performing a special action. Note: time in the rest of Minecraft also operates on "ticks," but a regular Minecraft ticks happen 20 times a second, making them twice as fast. This often confuses players who are aware of regular Minecraft ticks, so it's a good idea to note the difference here. Additionally, when we refer to "ticks" from here on out in this book, we are referring exclusively to Redstone ticks.

When you know how to use these and the many other rules of Redstone together you will be able to build incredible contraptions and systems, and the range of things you can do in everyone's favorite builder game expands in a huge way. In fact, Redstone is considered by many players to be the pinnacle of Minecraft knowledge, and many of the things that people build in the game that will cause less-experienced players to scratch their head and wonder how it even happened are made with Redstone.

THE COMPONENTS

Redstone is possible because of certain items and blocks in the game and the way they work together. In the next section, we'll look at each and every one of these very closely and give you all the details of how they work and what they're used in, but for now let's break the various Redstone components down into their most simple forms and talk about how they relate.

All Redstone items fall into one of the following categories:

1. Power & control components (usually just referred to as power components)
2. Transmission components
3. Mechanisms
4. Basic blocks
5. Rails and Rail-related items
6. Other items that interact with Redstone

In its most simple form, a Redstone build will have a power component and a mechanism, but most Redstone builds use items from at least three of these categories, and some can even use many items from all of these categories.

Let's take a second to get the basics of how the first three of these components interact with each other set in our minds. A typical simple Redstone build starts with a power component, which sends a power signal out. This is often carried by transmission components to either other Redstone circuits or to mechanisms. When mechanisms receive an ON power signal, they activate.

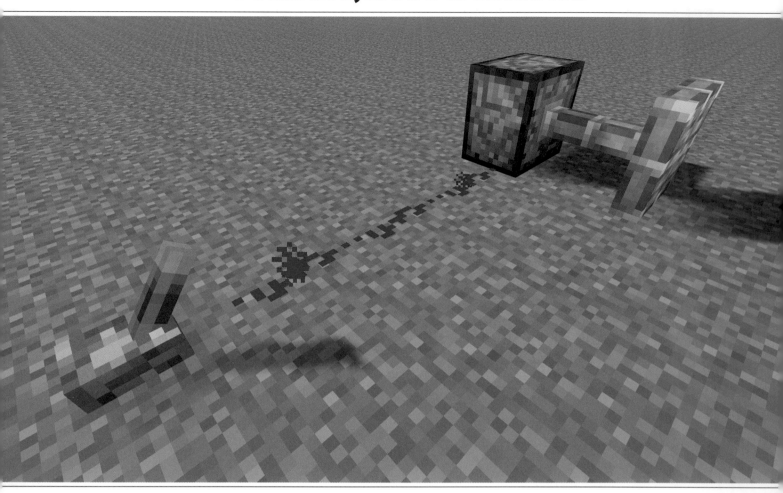

This is the basic Redstone setup: power component, wire and mechanism.

Somewhere in this process of sending a power signal from power component > transmission component > mechanism, the signal may interact with basic blocks of the game. What we mean by this is blocks that are usually used for building purposes, such as Cobblestone, Dirt, Wool, Glass, etc. There are two important types of blocks when it comes to Redstone, and they interact with Redstone in different ways:

Opaque blocks: "Opaque" is a word that means an object through which light does not travel. In Minecraft, this definition usually applies as well. Opaque blocks are important to Redstone because they can be powered by a Redstone signal. When a block is "powered," this means that a Redstone signal is going into it, and that Redstone mechanisms, as well as Repeaters and Comparators, will be activated by the block. This property of allowing Redstone signals to travel through themselves makes opaque blocks very important to Redstone.

Transparent blocks: As you might guess "transparent" blocks are typically those that can be "seen through" in the game, though this term also refers to a few such as Glowstone and Slabs that the game merely treats as transparent, though they themselves block vision. In terms of Redstone, transparent blocks are important because they do not take a Redstone power signal, even if one is going straight into them. This makes transparent blocks very useful to separate and block currents in Redstone building.

Some transparent blocks (left) and some opaque blocks (right).

Our final two types of Redstone items (Rail items, and other interactable blocks) are not nearly as core to Redstone concepts and building as the first four, though they can be integral parts of specific Redstone builds. These are essentially specialty items that can be used to create very specific results, as opposed to items that you'll be using in every build. All you really need to do now is to be aware that Rails and rail-related items as well as a few unique items can also interact with Redstone builds.

PUTTING IT ALL TOGETHER FOR THE FIRST TIME

Okay! So we know a bit about what Redstone is, we know a few of its rules, and we know the basic types of items that are used in Redstone builds, so it's time to actually test the stuff out!

We'll wrap this section up by doing some small Redstone placement, and talk a bit about what's happening with each thing we do. Open up your Minecraft, get a new world started in Creative Mode, and let's play with a little Redstone.

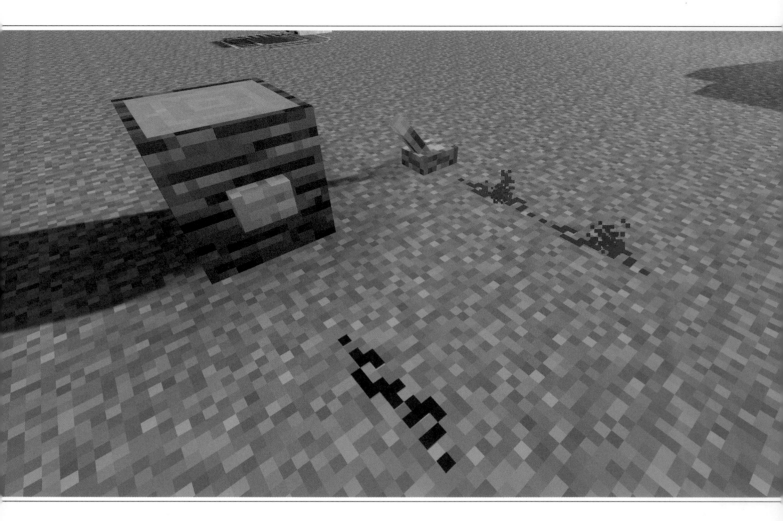

1. COMPONENT + REDSTONE DUST

First thing's first: let's see some Redstone actually powered up. Put a Lever, a Button (either kind) and some Redstone into your inventory. Place the Lever on the ground, and then place Redstone Dust on the ground right next to it. Now scoot over a bit and place the Button on a block (any opaque block is fine) and place Redstone Dust on the ground right in front of this. Make sure this second Dust is not touching the first and is not adjacent to the Lever. Now, activate the Lever. See how the Redstone Dust lights up when you flick the Lever? This means it's powered, and that the power state is constant. If you want to turn it OFF, just flip the Lever to the other state. Now press the Button. See the difference? For the Button, the Redstone was only powered for a brief moment, and then it went off. This example is just to show you how Redstone Dust can be powered, and that different power components power it differently (in this case a constant signal vs. a temporary one).

2. TRYING A MECHANISM

Now flip your Lever OFF, and then put a Piston into your inventory. Place the Piston down adjacent to the Redstone Dust you placed next to your Lever, and then flip the Lever ON. As you can see, as soon as you flip the Lever, the Piston will activate, extending. This is the simplest form of a Redstone build (perhaps your first ever!). All that's happening here is that the Lever is providing a signal, the Dust is carrying the signal to the Piston, and the Piston is recognizing that it is powered and is firing. Though most Redstone builds get much more complicated than this, essentially this is what is happening at the basic level in almost all Redstone creations.

3. POWERING AN OPAQUE BLOCK

Next, get a second Piston in your inventory, as well as a Redstone Torch and an opaque block. Move away from the Redstone items you have already placed, and put the opaque block down on the ground. Place a dot of Redstone Dust on the ground adjacent to the block (not on top of it though, for now), and then place the Redstone Torch on the opposite side of this Dust from the block. Now, go around to the opposite side of the block, and place the Piston down adjacent to this side of the block so that it is touching the block. For this example, make sure that the Piston is not adjacent to the Dust. You'll notice that the Piston also fires in this situation. This is because the block it is on is now "powered," which we talked about earlier in this chapter. The Redstone Torch, in this case, is providing the power signal to the Dust, which goes into the block and powers it, which then transfers the power to the mechanism. In this way we can see how powering blocks works and can be useful in Redstone.

4. MAKING THINGS MORE COMPLEX WITH A REPEATER

We're going to look at a very basic example of how we can make a Redstone build more complex for our final example. We'll need another Piston, another Lever and a Redstone Repeater for this one. Move away from your other Redstone builds, and place your Lever down on the ground. Put one dot of Redstone Dust adjacent to this Lever, and then stand on that Dust so that you are facing the opposite direction of the Lever. Aim down at the block on the opposite side of the Dust from the Lever while still standing on the Dust, and place your Repeater down. Now place the Piston on the block just after the Repeater, so you have a line of items that goes Lever>Dust>Repeater>Piston. Now flip the Lever. As you'll see, the Redstone current will go through the Dust, hit the Repeater, and then a slight amount of time later the Piston will fire. One of the features of Repeaters is that they output a signal at a slight delay, which in this case causes the Piston to fire, but which also has many other uses. We'll get to those later, but for now just notice how we can make the standard Redstone configuration more complex with other items.

Alrighty, we've done a little Redstone! That wasn't so bad, was it? Now you've got a bit of experience with the stuff, are starting to understand how it works, and hey! You can even tell your friends that you've started using Redstone. Good job miner!

YOUR FIRST 4 REDSTONE BUILDS

All this talk about the components and concepts and rules of Redstone has probably got you a bit overwhelmed, but don't worry: actually doing a little Redstone will help you tremendously in figuring out just what all that information means, as well as how to use it to make Minecraft even more awesome than it already is.

So, young Crafters, here's the part where we stop just telling you about Redstone and start actually makin' some cool stuff! These are your first five true Redstone builds, starting from the simplest Redstone doorbell and going through an awesome-lookin' Piston wave that's a great and easy way to impress those who don't have your Redstone skills.

These builds are designed to be super simple to build, in order to get you comfortable with using Redstone, yet they'll also teach you important lessons about Redstone and its properties. The builds also incorporate a few more complex properties and functions of Redstone, such as a NOT Gate and a clock, which you'll become much more familiar with later in the book as we get into more complex and difficult Redstone builds.

For now, however, we just want to focus on building the five contraptions here and understanding the simple basics of how they work. Later, we'll get into the more complex ideas behind some of the functions in these builds, but this chapter is all about dipping your toes into the world of Redstone in the simplest, most pain-free way possible. All you've got to do is follow the instructions and then recreate what you see in the images, and you'll already be on your way to earning your honorary Master's degree in Redstone Engineering.

Note: We recommend doing this in Creative Mode in order to learn these builds, but you can do them in Survival Mode as well if you have the materials.

THE DOORBELL

What it does: Lets ya know someone wants in your house by making a ding (or y'know, whatever weird noise you set it to).

How it works: A Note Block inside your home makes a noise when someone outside pushes a Button, powering the Note Block.

You'll Need: 1 Button, 1 Note Block, Redstone (optional)

Makin' a working, useful doorbell is just about the easiest Redstone project you'll ever do. In fact, it can be done without any Redstone Wire at all if you don't mind the Note Block being right inside your door. This is a good project to just get an idea of how power-giving items such as Buttons work with items like the Note Block that take power, and it's a cute little way to spruce up your home. Plus, Note Blocks can be heard up to 48 blocks from its location, so it will inform you of visitors even at a good distance.

1. Find the spot where you'd like to put the button that will activate your doorbell. Typically these are placed by a Door, but you could do it anywhere you wanted. For the easiest Doorbell, pick a spot on a wall near a Door that is one block off the ground and where the wall is just one block thick behind where the Button will be. Place the Button on this block.

2. Place the Note Block on the other side of the block that now has a Button on it.

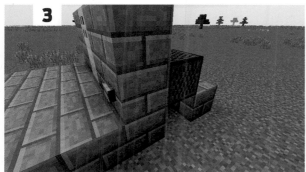

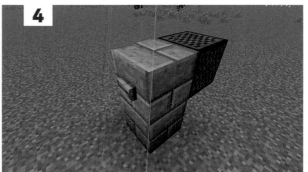

3. If the block under the Note Block is one you placed yourself, break it and leave the space empty. If you can't remember if you placed the block then go ahead and break it. This is done because the Note Block will change to a different sound than the beep we want if a human-placed block is underneath it.

4. Right-click the Note Block until it hits the note you'd like to use as your doorbell. This can be a little tricky, as sometimes the Note Block doesn't want to make noise, but just break the block and put it back down if you can't get it to work at first.

5. Press the Button back on the other side of the wall, and the Ncte Block will make its sound! The way this works is that the Button gives power to the block it is placed on, and this block gives power to the Note Block.

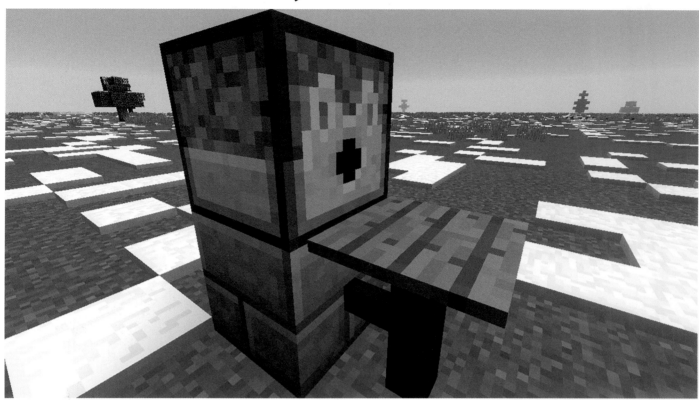

THE EASY POTION DISPENSER

What it does: Throws a Potion out at you when you run up and bump it (no need to click on this one).

How it works: A Dispenser is placed on a block, a Fence is placed in front of the block and Dispenser, and on top of the Fence is a Pressure Plate. When you run up to the Pressure Plate and push your crafter into it, it will press down, and whatever is in the Dispenser will launch out (Potions, in this case)

You'll Need: 1 Dispenser, 1 Fence, 1 Pressure Plate, 1 random block (optional, Dispenser could hang in the air), whatever Potions you want to dispense

Another quite simple little doohickey, the easy Potion dispenser makes taking Potions in Minecraft about as easy as it can be. Typically, you have to open your inventory or go to your hot bar and actually use a potion, or even run up to a Dispenser and push a Button or pull a Lever to get one to launch out at you. However, with the Easy Potion Dispenser, all you have to do is run up and bump the Pressure Plate, and you'll be smartly splashed with Potion.

1. Place a block of any kind down.

2. Put a Dispenser on top of this block.

3. Fill the Dispenser with a Potion of your choosing. This will actually work with anything a Dispenser can dispense at you, but Potions are one of the most useful options in this configuration.

4. Stand so the Dispenser is facing you (the side with the O-shaped hole) and look down at the block it is sitting on. Place one Fence on the block that is in front of this block that the Dispenser is on.

5. Place a Pressure Plate on top of the one Fence you have just placed.

6. Run up to the Pressure Plate, and it will press down and the Potion (or whatever else you've got in the Dispenser) will launch out. This is the Pressure Plate activating from interacting with your body and powering the Dispenser, which fires a random item inside of it at you.

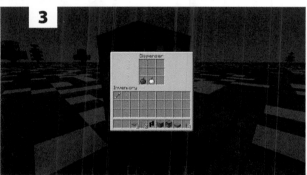

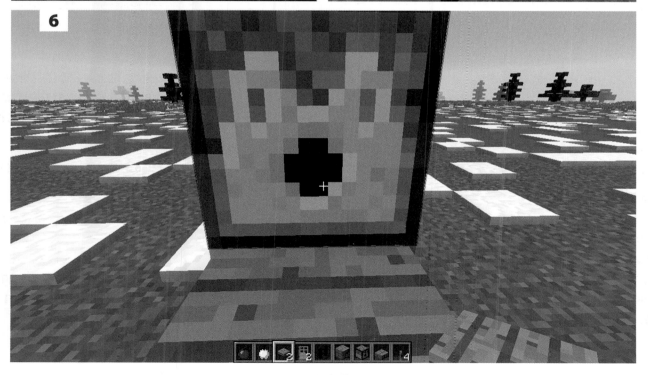

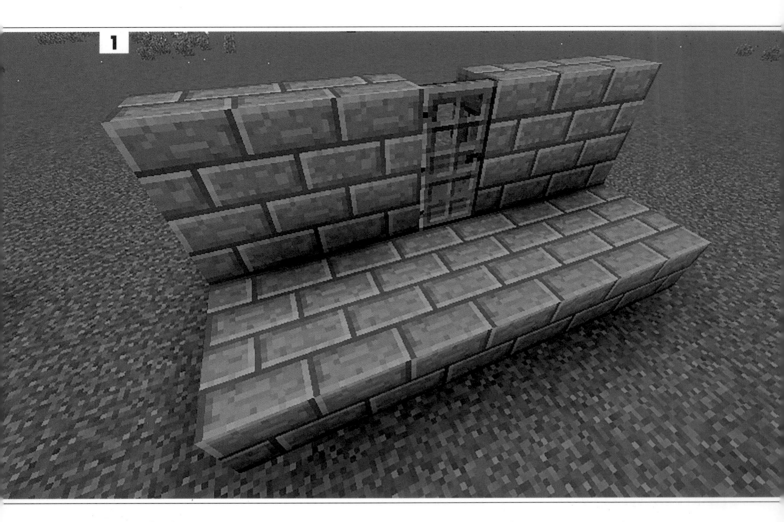

1

THE TRAPDOOR

What it does: Opens a hole in the ground wherever you'd like (in this case in front of a Door) at the flick of a Lever. Beneath this hole that opens is a big pit and/ or Lava, which anything that was standing on the block above the hole will fall into.

How it works: A Sticky Piston is attached to a block and extended over a pit, covering the hole. The Sticky Piston is attached underground to a Redstone "gate" called a Not Gate, which goes beneath the wall of a house using Redstone Wire. On the other side of the wall, a Lever on the ground surface turns the signal for the Redstone wire on and off, causing the Sticky Piston to expose and to cover the pit, alternatively. The whole contraption is hidden.

You'll Need: 1 Sticky Piston, 1 Lever, 1 Redstone Torch, 2 Redstone Wire, 2 Slabs of any kind, 1 random block

1. Find yourself a nice Door. This Door should be one which you would like to look out of, see a Creeper, and then kill that Creeper by making it drop to its doom. Also works with annoying players.

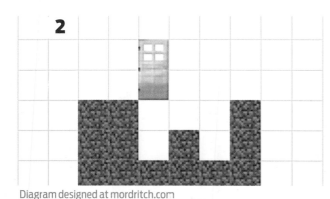

Diagram designed at mordritch.com

2. Dig out a pit in the pattern of Diagram 2. It should be only 1 block wide and 3 long, and it should alternate being 2 and 1 and then 2 blocks deep, as you also see in the Diagram.

3. Place a Redstone Torch on the wall as you see in the photo here.

4. Put a Sticky Piston in the space above the Redstone Torch facing toward the space in front of the Door (it will extend automatically), and then put a block of whatever type you'd like in front of the Sticky Piston. The 1 block deep hole in front of the Door should now be covered by the block stuck to the Sticky Piston.

5. Go to the other side of the wall which the Door is set in. Dig out a pit immediately on the other side of the wall from the block where the Sticky Piston and Redstone Torch are. Make this pit 1 block wide, 2 blocks long and 2 blocks deep, as in the picture.

6. Lay Redstone Wire down on the bottom of this pit. This is not essential to understand at this point, but what you have created in this section of the build is represented in Diagram 2.

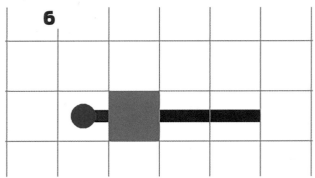

Diagram designed at mordritch.com

By adding a power source to the end of the Redstone Wire in Diagram 2 (or on a block above it, as we will do in the next step), we create what is called a NOT Gate. A NOT Gate is a type of construction known as a logic gate, which manipulates a Redstone signal.

7. Cover the last block of the pit (farthest from the wall) with the same type of block that makes up the rest of the floor. Put a Lever on top of this block. Now cover the second block of the pit with the same type of block, but with no Lever.

8. Flip the Lever and the Sticky Piston should pull back and uncover the hole in front of the Door.

9. Go back through the Door to the pit in front of it, and dig the pit deeper. Here you have a few options: place Lava or Cactus at the bottom of the pit to kill intruders with damage, make a long drop that will kill the intruder (at least 24 blocks down for a TKO), or build an area at the bottom for the intruders to fall into and just, y'know, hang out. Until you come to slice them up with your Sword, of course.

10. Go back up and cover up the Sticky Piston by placing 2 Slabs of any kind on top of the two blocks it takes up. Don't put one over the spot in front of the door, of course.

11. Wait for a Creeper to come stand outside your door, flip the Lever, profit.

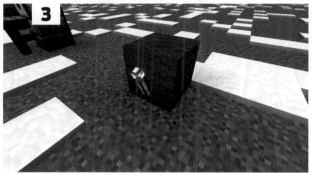

THE SIMPLEST CLOCK

What it does: Creates a pulse of Redstone power that turns on and off at a regular interval, which allows many concepts to be created with Redstone, including but not limited to contraptions that keep time.

How it works: A Redstone Torch powers a Redstone Repeater, which slows down the signal slightly (in this case it is a '4 tick' delay). After 4 ticks the power goes through the Repeater and on to the Wire after it, which curves around to power the block that the original Redstone Torch was on. This turns off the Redstone Torch temporarily, in turn turning off the signal through the Redstone Repeater after 4 more ticks. This repeats indefinitely unless acted upon from an outside signal.

You'll Need: 1 Redstone Torch, 1 Redstone Repeater, 3 Redstone Wire, 1 Random Block

When referring to Redstone components, a "clock" is a Redstone construction that alternately causes an on signal and then an off signal to be transmitted from itself every so many seconds in a constant pulse.

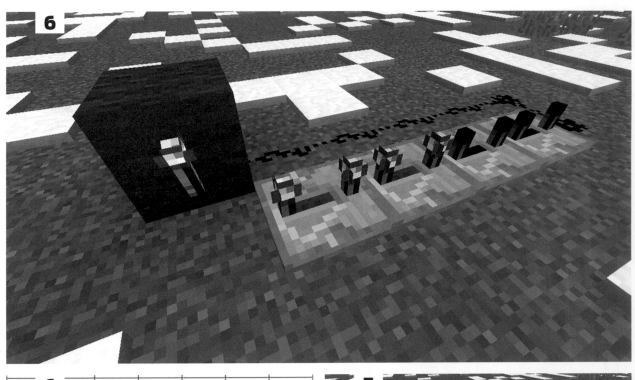

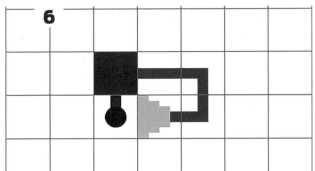

Diagram designed at mordritch.com

Clocks are power loops, where a signal is transmitted from a power source, slowed down by Repeaters (or other ways, in more complex cases), and then is sent back to the original power source, temporarily turning it off. This causes the power to pulse with a consistent amount of time between each pulse, and the amount of time between each pulse can be customized by the builder through using multiple Repeaters in a row as well as other tactics.

This pulsing signal can be used to give something else power for a few ticks, and then take it away. So for instance, a Piston hooked up to a clock would continuously extend and pull back as long as it was hooked up to the clock.

This is the simplest version of a clock, and it's quite useful for everything from practical, mechanical Redstone builds to the most complex logic circuits.

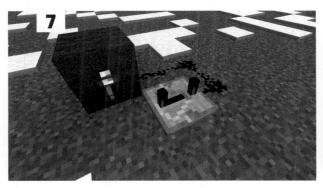

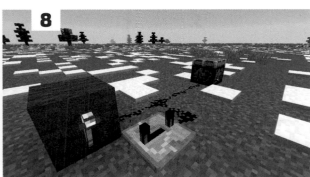

1. Turn so that the direction you would like your power to go in is to your right. Make sure there are about five blocks of usable ground space to your right (if there is not, scooch over a bit so there is).

2. Place your random block down. This has to be one that can transfer power, so something like Stone, Wool or Wood of any type is good.

3. Keeping the direction you would like the signal to move in to your right, place a Redstone Torch on the side of the block facing you, as in the image.

4. As in the image, place a Redstone Repeater on the block to the right of the block that your Redstone Torch hangs over (so, caddy-corner to the block the Redstone Torch is on).

5. Set this repeater on the last setting (4 ticks). This is important- Redstone Torches cannot take a signal that is too fast coming back into them, and Redstone Torches will burn out after a while if you have too quick of a signal piping into them (turn your Repeater to a faster signal when your clock is fully built and test it out sometime, just to see this happen). The reason for this is somewhat complex, but all you need to know at this point is that you need to slow this signal down a bit with your Repeater.

6. Copy the Redstone pattern from the Diagram, taking it one block on the ground past the repeater. then both blocks on the ground to the right of the block you have a Torch on.

7. If you have set the Repeater to the right delay in step #5, your clock will start working immediately, doing a pulsing signal.

8. To use your clock, just put 1 Redstone Wire branching off of the existing Redstone Wire in the clock. You can then extend this to whatever you want to power.

Tips!

You can put a Lever on the side of the block in your Redstone clock, and you can turn the clock on and off with the Lever.

You can create clocks with greater delays (much greater, theoretically) by using more Redstone Repeaters in a row.

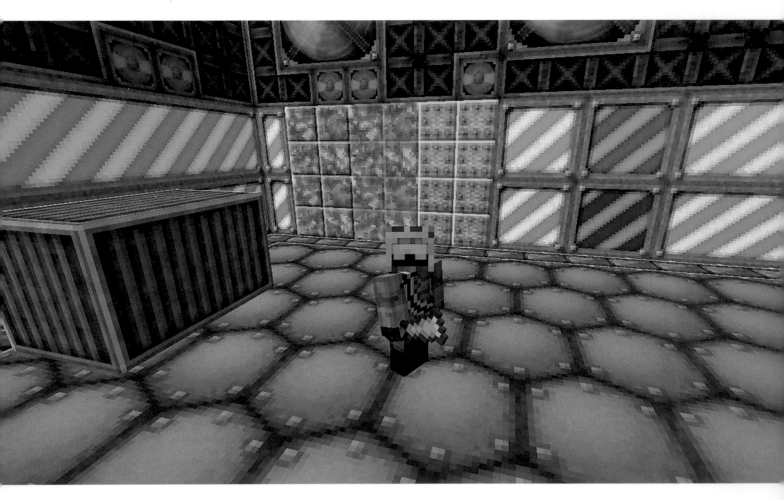

MASTER THE MODS

It's always said that what you can do in Minecraft is limited only by your imagination. This is true, but only to a point. While you certainly can build just about anything you can think of in the regular game, which is often called "vanilla" Minecraft, the palette of blocks and items that you can use to build your creations is limited to what comes with the game. Sure you can combine them together to make them look similar to almost anything, but what if you had more to use, more to choose from? What could you create then, if you truly had no limits?

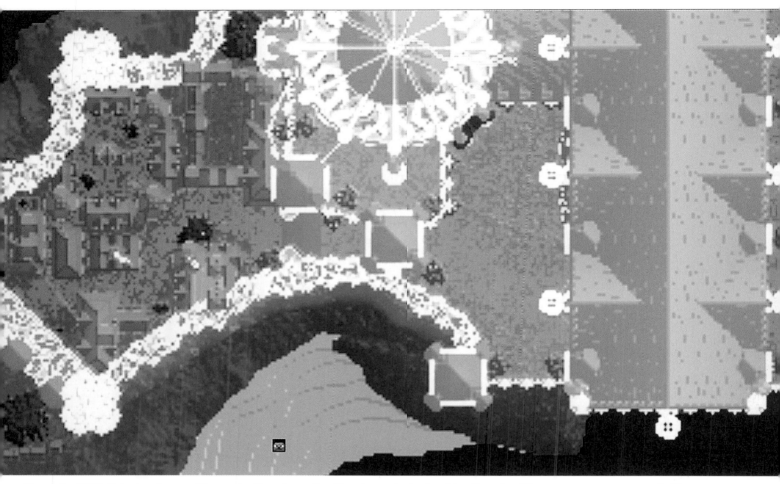

Opposite: With this chapter, you'll soon be like player Drullkus here, decked out in all sorts of fancy new gear surrounded by a heap of new, awesome blocks. Above: See the world of Minecraft like never before, sometimes quite literally like with this minimap mod called VoxelMap.

THE WORLD OF MODS

That we even can answer that question is because of one of the best, not-all-that-secret secrets in gaming: There is another facet of Minecraft outside of the vanilla game that adds these extra items and truly does turn the game into whatever the human mind can come up with, and it is accessible to any player. Millions of Minecrafters are already taking advantage of this fascinating, thrilling semi-secret world within Minecraft, and in fact, if you've ever been on a Minecraft server and wondered how the heck they got all those crazy new blocks or how they do things like let you play paintball in Minecraft, you were actually taking part in it without even knowing it.

We're talking about the world of Minecraft "mods," a term that is short for modifications and which refers to code created by fans and inserted into the regular game. Mods are designed to add amazing new features to change Minecraft in an incredibly wide variety of ways, each of which came entirely from the imagination of players just like you and all of which are super cool in the unique ways that they change the game.

Mods can let you do everything from build a rocketship and fly to the moon, to going deep into ancient pyramids to battle mighty Egyptian queens with your magic Bow in mods like Atum.

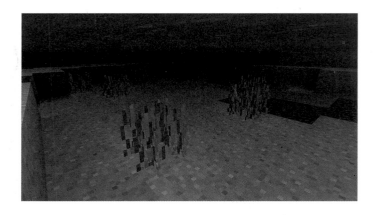

WHAT CAN MODS DO?

These changes can be just about anything, from new items and blocks to new mobs to fight to whole new, fully-realized ways to play the game. Want to have a realistic gunfight in a fully-decked out Wild West world in Minecraft? Want to fly a plane around a roaring tornado that's ripping up a mighty mountain range, in Minecraft? Want to battle forty-block-tall monsters by casting blistering and crackling magic spells from the walls of a fantasy-land castle, populated with its own denizens? Want to turn into a hamster and fly to space in a rocket?

You can do all of that and more with mods.

FAVORITE MOD SPOTLIGHT!

Agrarian Skies

In one sentence: A mod that takes the Skyblock challenge of Minecraft and adds in a ton of mods and a questing system that all works together to create an epic survival adventure while also teaching you many of the most beloved mods.

Webpage: http://bit.ly/AgrarianSkiesPage

Complexity Level: 5 Diamonds
Adds Items?: Yes
Adds Mobs?: No

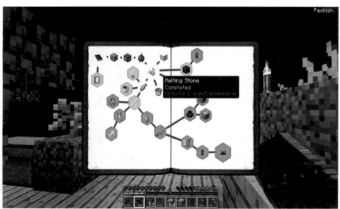

Mods are awesome: that, we think most everyone would agree on. However, since mods add so much new stuff and change up the game so extensively, it can be super overwhelming to fire one up and see all this new stuff you don't know how to mess with. Many mods come with little in-game Books that you can open up and read, but trying to remember all the things you read and switching back and forth between them and actually playing is pretty darn hard, even for the best Crafters.

We suggest that if you're looking to actually learn how to do some of the amazing things in mods like all of the Tinkers' mods, Thaumcraft, Thermal Expansion, or Applied Energistics, check out the Agrarian Skies modpack. Actually a super, super modded version of Skyblock and available on the FTB Launcher, Agrarian Skies puts you in a world where you have very little to start with, but all of the things you need to eventually build everything in the mods it contains. It uses a very well-done and inventive questing system to teach you how to do a ton of the stuff in these mods by making them goals, and it does so in a way that's both hugely entertaining and also quite challenging. If we had to pick, Agrarian Skies would be our very favorite modpack of all.

FEX'S RANDOM STUFF MOD

Creator: FEX___96

In one sentence: Like it says, this mod adds a bunch of random new craftable items, including computers and TVs, robots, food, weapons and a bunch of household stuff.

Version: 1.7.10
Installed Through: Forge (manually)
Where you can find it:
http://fexcraft.net/downloads.html

Complexity Level: 3 Diamonds
Adds Items?: Yes
Adds Mobs?: Sort-of, supposedly has one without a texture

Fex's Random Stuff Mod, or FRSM, has all sorts of items to add to your Minecraft experience, and as the name says, the types of stuff it adds is pretty darn random. Like, for instance, tiny model trains aren't really something that we ever were *looking* to have in Minecraft, but why not!

One of the things FRSM does best is to add a bunch of modern household-style items like TVs, washing machines, computers and a heap of foods like someone might find in their refrigerator. It makes for the ability to really stock up and enliven homes that have a more contemporary look, where before there was definitely a bit of anachronism with modern-looking houses having a bunch of medieval stuff in them.

EXTRABIOMESXL

Creator: ExtrabiomesXL Team

In one sentence: Another mod with a plethora of very well-designed biomes run by a team thoroughly committed to creating the best mod it can.

Version: 1.5.2, 1.7.10
Installed Through: Forge (manually)
Where you can find it:
http://bit.ly/ExtrabiomesXLMod

Complexity Level: 2 Diamonds
Adds Items?: Yes
Adds Mobs?: No

The team behind ExtrabiomesXL is among the best when it comes to taking what it does seriously and really giving the community of modders something amazing. This mod is another that simply adds a ton of great biome content to vanilla 'Craft, with over 25 painstakingly designed and well-updated biomes to give your Minecraft world a little more ecological oomph. The folks working on this have really done their research on environments, and it comes across in their work with excellent generation algorithms for environs like marshes, redwood forests, and the rocky alpine biome.

THE TWILIGHT FOREST

Creator: Benimatic

In one sentence: A new, fantastical dimension of glimmering dusk adventures through a magical forest, complete with fascinating creatures, an adventure to follow and all manner of new plants and blocks to discover.

Version: 1.7.10 and way back
Installed Through: Forge (manually) or through the FTB Launcher
Where you can find it:
http://bit.ly/TwilightForestPage

Complexity Level: 3.5 Diamonds
Adds Items?: Yes
Adds Mobs?: Yes

The Twilight Forest mod is one of our very favorites, as it is just so darn enchanting. As opposed to other biome mods, this one is not just randomly created in the world; you actually have to build a portal to it and jump in. Once you do that, you'll find yourself surrounded by what might be the most aesthetically wonderful realm in all of modded Minecraft, with its own set of biomes and areas, not to mention unique mobs and things to experience. It truly is the premier fantasy environment in Minecraft, and it feels like you just stepped into the pages of a 1970s fantasy adventure novel, or the land of the movie *Legend*.

Once you do step into this perpetual twilight land, you'll notice immediately that everything is different. Deer and Fireflies and Bighorns roam the land, and the towering trees are not even a bit like the ones from regular Minecraft. There is also much to fear in this new world, which will throw over a dozen new hostile mobs at you, such as the Kobold and Swarm Spider or bosses like the Naga, Hydra, and Lich.

There is a bit of an RPG element to the story of this land, as well as to its aesthetic, as it is set up to have a progression from boss to boss, and the land itself is designed to draw you through these progressions. Along the way you'll find well over a hundred new blocks and items to mine, manipulate, craft and master, all with a fantasy bent and totally fun to discover. It is a beautiful place and a beautiful mod, and it's one every Crafter who has ever been interested in fantasy should check out.

FERULLO'S GUNS MOD

Creator: Ferullo

In one sentence: Another old one, this is perhaps the primary gun-adding mod for Minecraft, adding many realistic guns to the game.

Version: 1.6.4
Installed Through: Forge (manually)
Where you can find it:
http://bit.ly/FerullosGunsMod

Complexity Level: 2 Diamonds
Adds Items?: Yes
Adds Mobs?: No

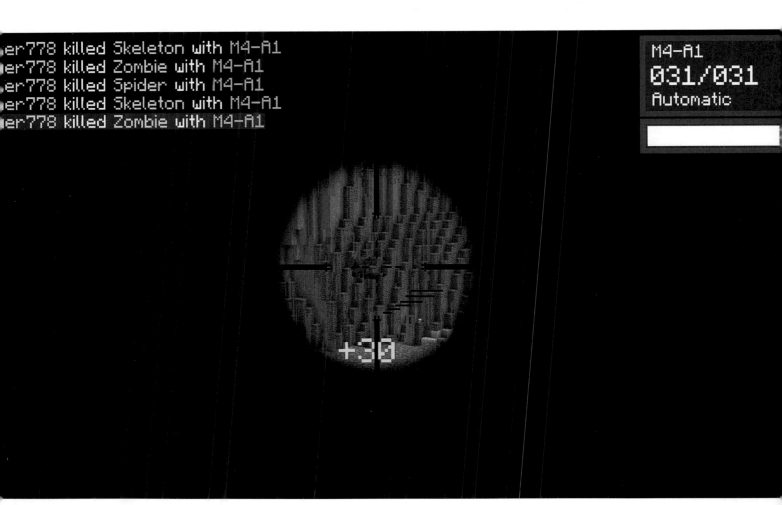

er778 killed Skeleton with M4-A1
er778 killed Zombie with M4-A1
er778 killed Spider with M4-A1
er778 killed Skeleton with M4-A1
er778 killed Zombie with M4-A1

M4-A1
031/031
Automatic

+30

Mod creator Ferullo has switched his efforts over to a new *Counter-Strike*-based mod for Minecraft , but his old Guns Mod is still one of the most commonly found and frequently downloaded mods that takes our tame lil Minecraft and adds all sorts of things that go "boom!" and "pew!" to it. The number of guns this thing adds is pretty tremendous, with many styles based on all sorts of real guns like high-caliber sniper rifles, ACOGs, M-16s and so much more, plus it even throws in some fun stuff like night vision goggles and realistic body armor. If you'd like to make your Crafting a bit more mature and dangerous, and especially if you dig games like *Call of Duty* or *Counter-Strike,* Ferullo's Guns Mods is your go-to. Oh, and if you like the idea of zombies + guns, check out the Crafting Dead mod, which uses this Guns Mod, but adds in a whole zombie apocalypse thing!

MILLÉNAIRE

Creator: Kinniken

In one sentence: Adds five new types of Villages to Minecraft, each of which has its own culture and an extensive amount of new items and Villager types, and which can grow, trade and interact with the player in a large number of ways.

Version: 1.7.2, 1.7.10
Installed Through: Forge (manually) or through the Millénaire mod installer
Where you can find it:
http://millenaire.org/

Complexity Level: 3.5 Diamonds
Adds Items?: Yes
Adds Mobs?: Yes

The basic idea of Millénaire is simple, but in actuality this is one of the more complex and comprehensive mods out there, so much so that it would almost be a total conversion mod if it weren't otherwise set in vanilla Minecraft. The core concept is that there are various cultures of Villagers around the Minecraft world in randomly generated Villages, and these Villagers all have jobs like mining or chopping Wood (instead of just milling about). There is a leader, a trading hall and there are many ways to interact with the Villages, including helping them get items they need to build their Village and taking quests from them.

On top of this, you can also gain a reputation with these Villages and even become a leader, which in turn allows you the option to build your own Village that you can control (in terms of what they do and build). The Creation Quest you can get from the Villages is also a pretty big change to the game, as it adds in a little backstory for the Minecraft world and sends the player on an epic quest to gather items and information. All-in-all, Millénaire is a way to really spice up and populate the regular Minecraft world, turning it into more of an RPG builder game with a plot and characters, as opposed to being just about what the player wants to do. It's very cool, and one of the best ways to bring excitement back into the game if you're a little bored with regular Crafting.

MINECRAFT COMES ALIVE

Creator: WildBamaBoy and SheWolfDeadly

In one sentence: Another Villager mod, but this one is more about tweaking existing Villagers so they can be more intricately interacted with and so that they look and behave in a wider variety of ways.

Version: 1.6.4, 1.7.2, 1.7.10
Installed Through: Forge (manually), requires both MCA and the RadixCore
Where you can find it:
http://www.radix-shock.com/mca--overview.html, http://bit.ly/MinecraftComesAliveCurse"

Complexity Level: 3 Diamonds
Adds Items?: Yes
Adds Mobs?: Yes

Catrina the Child

an turn off these messages at the Main Menu.
t Mods->Minecraft Comes Alive->Config->Tutorial mode->false.

a the Child: Why, hello there!
he Child: Hey, what's going on?

Villagers are loud, annoying, almost useless little creatures in vanilla Minecraft (okay, they're pretty adorable too), and it always seems like you should be able to interact with them a lot more than you can. Where Millénaire is all about economy and interacting with Villagers on a bigger scale, Minecraft Comes Alive is about Villager personalities and having relationships with them. It replaces the strange-nosed, squawking brown Villager models that don't do much with a whole heap of Villager skins (about 200 of them!) that are much more human, and it changes the shape of Villages to be much more realistic.

Even better, you can now click on Villagers and interact with them in dozens of ways, including flirting, talking and even hiring them to do jobs! Each Villager has its own specialization, like farming or guarding, and its own personality, and they remember your interactions with them. You can become friends or, if you get close enough, even marry one. There are literally thousands of dialogue options with Villagers in Minecraft Comes Alive, and while it's not the world-changer that Millénaire is, it's probably the best semi-vanilla Minecraft mod for Villagers out there.

PIXELMON

In one sentence: Turns Minecraft into a 3D first-person Pokémon game, with just about everything you'd hope for from such a mod.

Approximate Mod Count: 1, except in versions where it is bundled with other mods
Complexity Level: 3 Diamonds

Adds Items?: Yes
Adds Mobs?: Yes

It's no secret that Pokémon is one of the most popular and long-lasting game series of all time, so the fact that the hardcore modding community for Minecraft has gone out and recreated Pokémon inside of their own game or that it's the most popular Technic mod should be no big shock to anyone. Pixelmon is just that mod, and to answer your questions: Yes, there are Pokémon wandering around; yes, you can catch them; yes, you can fight them with trainers and other players; and yes, it all works.

Though you can just load this one up through the Technic launcher and play in your own world, we'd also suggest jumping on one of the official servers (just go to multiplayer instead of single player, and they're listed) where people have actually gone so far as to build functioning Pokémon Centers, gyms, and even the Elite Four! Plus, you can show off your sick Mewtwo and find hundreds of other players to battle with. This one's a treat, whether you're a longtime Pokémon fan or just like the idea of a bunch of adorable battle creatures wandering around your Minecraft home.

Note: there are quite a few versions of Pixelmon out there, as well as a lot of knock-offs, so make sure you're downloading the one you want when you go looking for it.

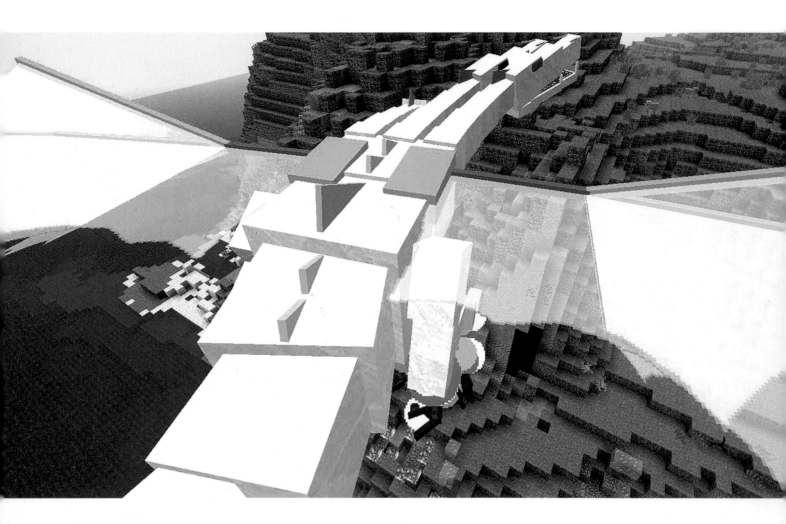

ORESPAWN

Creator: TheyCallMeDanger, MeganLorraine, and the Orespawn team

In one sentence: Orespawn is a polished honker of a mod that adds a ton of everything to Minecraft, including mobs, items, blocks, systems, biomes, dimensions, new things to do, and really just too much to list.

Version: 1.6.4, 1.7.10
Installed Through: Forge (manually)
Where you can find it:
http://www.orespawn.com/

Complexity Level: 5 Diamonds
Adds Items?: Yes
Adds Mobs?: Yes

One of our biggest modpacks in the book, Orespawn is a comprehensive total overhaul of the game in just about every way. It contains mods with focuses on armor and weapons, tons of new mobs and bosses, at least half a dozen new dimensions to travel to, gardening, building, dozens of new plants and trees and even, oddly enough, the ability to get a girlfriend in the game.

The best way to really get a feel for what Orespawn can do to transform your game (and it will transform it, inside and out) is to play it, but the second best would be to take a look at the list of "Things to Do" Orespawn lists in its guides on its website. Here's a little excerpt of some of the most interesting and oddest entries on that list, to whet your appetite to play this most excellent mod:

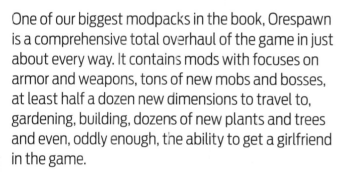

- **Fight Mobzilla.** Or just watch him as he destroys the entire Village Dimension...

- **Ride a Hoverboard!**

- **Build yourself a home in the Crystal Dimension.** Stay awake and watch the chaos!

- **BUILD A ZOO!!!!!** Don't forget to use the ZooKeeper Items on your critters!

- **Plant a garden** with moth plants and some torches in the Utopia Dimension. Kick your feet up and relax a bit.

- **Make a dance floor** under an Experience tree and stay up late dancing with your Girlfriend.

- **Defeat a few of the major mobs:** Water Dragon, Basilisc, Emperor Scorpion, Alien's little brother, Robo-Warrior, Kyuubi...

- **Ride a Cephadrome at night,** really slow, really low. It's like riding a mob-mower!

- **Find a Basilisc maze,** and get through it without cheating.

- **Make a bag of Popcorn.**

- **Make a Corn Dog!**

- **Mine some rubies and make yourself a Thunderstaff!**

- **Ride a Giant Spider Robot!!!!!**

10 AWESOME BUILDS

P.I.E. PLANT INVESTIGATION EXPERIMENTS
By: CrashCraftPro (VigourBuilds)

P.I.E. isn't a building, it's a machine, and one with a story and a purpose. The P.I.E. is designed to travel the world and reside temporarily where there are rare plants, on which its massive frame does experiments in order to try and find a way to save the world. Alternatively, its crew of 6 technicians and scientists is trying to find a plant that can produce more oxygen to use in a space station, so that the people of Earth can leave their doomed planet. With the apocalypse still decades away, P.I.E. spends 10 years in each location before moving on to the next, and in the interim its precious cargo and expensive frame is protected by 15 mini helicopters from would-be raiders. Perhaps even more impressive than the thoroughly rich and unique concept for this build is that it was created by one single builder using no outside software, something rare for a build of this size and detail.

AVARICIA
By: Schnogot

Good jumpin' jackrabbits this is a pretty build. The cohesiveness and balance of the overall design is astounding to begin with, but it's in the decorative details like the many arches, buttresses, the texturing on the walls and the use of the green as a secondary color bring this build from great to stupendous. If that weren't enough, the innards of this city are just as painstakingly crafted, as is the "wild beach" and the island-dotted lake that it features. Even cooler, it's set up to be a PvP map with a secret treasure, with the idea being that 24 people take each other on in this map while seeking treasure and weapons. Only one can leave, and as Schnogot asks on Planet Minecraft, "Will it be you?"

CLOUDHAVEN
By: lynchyinc

Cityships are another genre of building that you'll see here and there on Minecraft sites, as is steampunk (something you'll see all the time), but CloudHaven is almost definitely the most jam-packed ship we've ever seen that still looks like it was professionally designed. It almost looks like a creature, like some sort-of fish robot swimming through the sky, but in the "reality" of the build it's an old mining ship that, after a catastrophe known as the "Void Storm" took away all of the land in the world, CloudHaven was converted to a cityship with other 1000 "traders, skylords, merchants, smugglers, pirates and proletariat alike" living on it. There is a cool set of challenges associated with this map, mostly based around trying to survive and finding things in the ship like the treasury room, which is a cool twist on the standard steampunk sky map.

ELBANE'S ARRIVAL
By: MrD4nny

Right so, the very first time we loaded up Elbane's Arrival, we didn't really know how big the dragon (the one the name Elbane belongs to) in it would be, or where it would be. When we turned around and had this huge thing loading up right behind us, all fangs and glowing eyes, it actually put literal fear into us. Feeling something that big right behind you, even virtually, is pretty dang freaky. That should tell you all you need to know to want to check this build out, but there's more to it as well. Elbane is attacking a city called Desnig on a floating air island, which is well designed itself and lends an excellent sense of drama to the build.

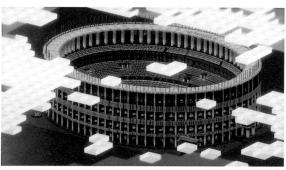

ROMECRAFT COLOSSEUM
By: stugace

A perfect ellipse built with cubes? Yep, that's the Romecraft Colosseum, a build that was meant to be as close to a real life colosseum as possible, and which draws heavy influence from the Colosseum in Rome (note, there are two correct spellings for this type of building). This build is 189x156x48 blocks and has 456 outer support columns, and the builders were so concerned with being accurate to ancient Roman structures that they take the time on their Planet Minecraft page to point out that, while the Rome Colosseum had pillars 4m thick, this build was forced to make theirs 3m thick due to not being able to make round shapes in Minecraft. Regardless, it is a remarkably accurate representation of an ancient, famous structure, and it looks quite striking with shaders on.

SAILOR'S HIDEOUT
By: Shady og Ola

We just can't say enough for a good, small build put in just the right place and done just the right way. Sailor's Hideout, with its frame that would be diminutive in a regular Minecraft landscape but which stands out tremendously against the flat ocean setting on which it exists, is one such build. Its creator calls it a "relaxed build" and invites the player to "settle down and enjoy the environment," and when you combine that sentiment with its telling name, you can really get a feel for the mood of this build. It's a place for hard-working sailors who have braved the dangers of the deep to come and take some time off, maybe because they need to get out from under

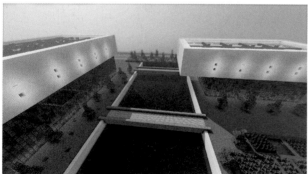

CONTEMPORARY MUSEUM
By: Joueur_inconnu

This is one of our favorite builds by one of our favorite builders. It pulls off the fascinating trick of looking almost exactly like its real-life counterparts (that being modern museums), which in Minecraft's blocky world is quite hard to do indeed. It's also a great mash-up of modern and ancient architecture in a way that absolutely makes sense, as well as a tremendous lesson in architecture itself and compound design. The creator uses water perfectly, and each building is laid out to specific dimensions. We wouldn't be surprised to hear that Joueur_inconnu is a real-life architect or has some training in the field, and this kind of build shows that Minecraft can be used as a tool for training in such fields as design and architecture. Really though, who could say blocky buildings and straight lines are boring after looking at this? An absolutely beautiful build.

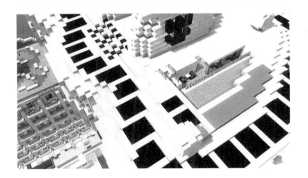

OASIS OF THE SEAS TERMINAL 18

By: CharlesGoldburn

CharlesGoldburn is almost unquestionably Minecraft's premier cruise boat builder. Among his many, many boats he has painstakingly recreated in Minecraft in a 1:1 scale (meaning they are as big in Minecraft as they are in real life) is the Oasis of the Seas boat, in this build seen at a docking terminal. Goldburn's boats are all recreations of real boats, and what makes them special versus the many, many other cruise boat recreations out there is that he goes above and beyond to detail these boats realistically. Just check out that above shot: you can see everything from deck chairs to bars to realistic railing! These ships are fully complete from outside to in, meaning there is virtual space for all of the 6300 passengers and 2394 crew in the 16 decks of the Oasis, a ship that is classified as the largest class of cruise ship in the world.

INFAMOUS
By: The NewHeaven team

The video game Infamous is the inspiration for this, one of the most colorful and creative city builds we've ever seen in the game. There is much to see in this build, which goes for quite a ways, and what makes it special versus other city builds (besides the extremely high skill of the builders themselves, which is obvious from the moment you step into this creation) is that the fantastical world of the video game that it comes from allows its builders to pull from the best parts of reality and imagination to create something that is better than both. It's truly excellent, with surprises quite literally around every corner, and it is one of those that has hours worth of exploration contained within its wide bounds.

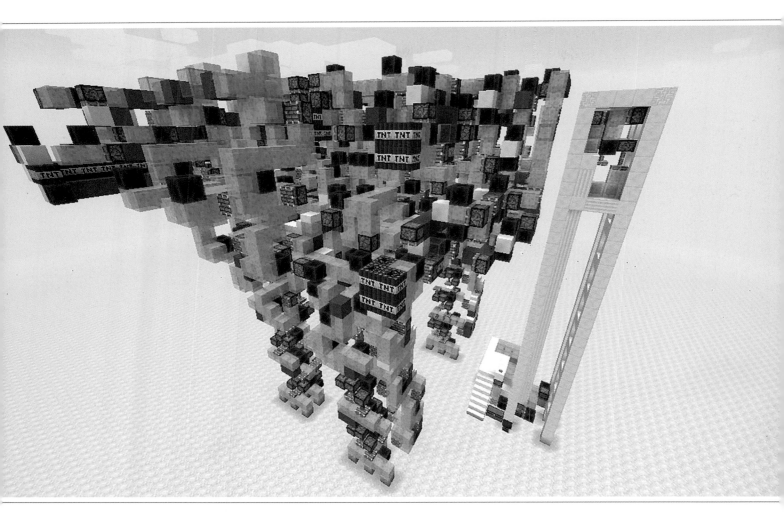

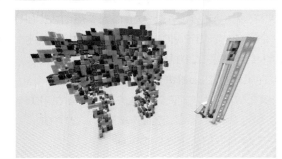

MEGA GARGANTUA
By: Cubehamster

Another build by a true master of Redstone, this time we have a build by the weird genius Cubehamster that's so odd it'd almost be comical if it weren't horrifying in its size and movement. This build is the Mega Gargantua, a shuffling Redstone cannon-laden robot that will start a slow trek across the lands when activated by a player in the driver's spot. As it moves, you can run about lighting the cannons and blowing the crap out of the countryside, moving down area after area as your enormous robo-steed trundles along under its own power. This build is done using the magic of the Slimeblock, whose introduction into Minecraft allowed for the first self-moving vehicles in the game. Cubehamster, a veteran of the Redstone scene and a Redstone magician with a love for complex moving builds, says that they went through over 1200 versions of this build getting it right, 90% of which didn't work at all.

THE FUTURE OF MINECRAFT

The future is coming! At least, that is, the future of Minecraft, and with it there look like there are going to be some major new additions to the ways that people play this game that's really not-so-little anymore.

The two big things to expect in the upcoming years that could well change everything about gaming as a whole, not just Minecraft, but which especially should excite Minecraft fans are access to personal servers and virtual reality.

PERSONAL SERVERS

So playing Minecraft alone is pretty fun, but we all know that getting on a server with dozens, hundreds or even thousands of other players is like nothing else. Players that are fortunate and, often, good enough at computers know that it goes one step beyond this: the best way to play Minecraft is to have a server with all of your friends on it that you can keep for years and years. In fact, many of the best Minecraft creations that you see in this book and around the internet were made on servers just like this, and it's how a lot of builders get really, seriously good at the game.

The thing is though; setting up a server is hard on your own. But, these days, two new services are lining up to make difficult server maintenance and setup a thing of the past!

One is Minecraft Realms, a service run by Mojang itself that allows up to 10 players to join a private server without doing any setup of their own at all. This doesn't cost much and is by far the easiest and most reliable way to get your own Minecraft server.

The other option, though, is even more powerful, and that is the many different services online that you can now pay to create and maintain a server for you. There are many of these, and just Googling "Minecraft Servers" will bring up a whole list of companies offering this service, often for as little as less than $10 a month (depending on what kind of server you want). What's even cooler is that you can really pick what you want with these, including mods and different mini-games! It's very cool, and makes connecting with your friends through Minecraft easy as pie.

VIRTUAL REALITY

With its first-person perspective and huge popularity, Minecraft has been one of the first games to get tested extensively on the newfangled virtual reality, or VR, headsets that have been making their way into the world in the last few years. Many of these headsets are on the verge of being released for home computers and consoles like the PlayStation 4, and you can bet that Minecraft will be one the most popular games to play using them. Can you imagine actually feeling like you're walking through that giant castle you built, or dodging Skeleton arrows flying right at your face? How fun!

Even more interesting, perhaps, is Microsoft's own entry into the new world of headsets and virtual reality, called the HoloLens. This headset is actually being marketed as something specifically to use with Minecraft, and it works a little different than other VR. Instead of going inside the view of the Minecraft world, what the HoloLens will do is to show you the world around you, but project your Minecraft world onto it. So, for instance, you could set a table as the surface,

and then you can actually have the house you built in the game show up there in 3D. You can see characters moving around and even interact with them! Or, use a wall as the surface, and you'll open up a window into your world to peer into.

The future is going to be absolutely amazing you guys!

HEROES OF MINECRAFT

With Minecraft being such a very popular game, and with so many incredible things having been done in the game, it's no surprise that there are a few Crafters out there whose skills and abilities make them special players of the game. We're talking about some seriously amazing Minecrafters, whether they're masters of Redstone, map builders extraordinaire, owners of popular servers, or just plain famous personalities in the game.

Though this list is far from comprehensive, here are some of the Minecrafters we love for their achievements in the game, which we think are so darn cool that they make these players Heroes of Minecraft.

To get the full effect here, you need to know that what looks like the ground is actually the wall. Yep: you're falling right now!

Another angle of the awesome bedroom level. Note: that bed is quite a lot bigger than most houses people build in the game.

BIGRE

Specialty: Creative maps, especially puzzle maps

Can be found at: bit.ly/bigremap

Bigre is a map creator best known for his wildly popular mini-game map called The Dropper, which features various highly decorated areas that players must fall through without hitting anything. In fact, The Dropper is by far the most downloaded map on the biggest Minecraft map repository (PlanetMinecraft.com), where it has been downloaded over 1 million times. In addition to The Dropper and its sequel, Bigre has also created a number of other mini-games, maps and even a resource pack. Though he's not quite as prolific or high profile as many of the others on this list, the importance of this map to the community and the creativity Bigre puts into their builds makes them one of our Minecraft Heroes.

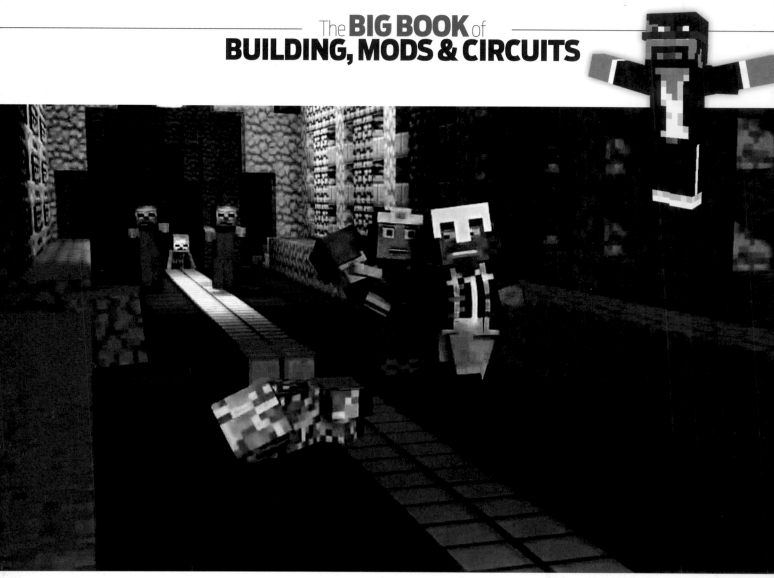

A shot from CaptainSparklez's "Fallen Kingdom" music video, a parody of Coldplay's "Viva la Vida" done Minecraft style.

CAPTAINSPARKLEZ

Specialty: Let's Play Minecraft videos on YouTube, also MC related music videos

Can be found at:
YouTube- bit.ly/CaptainSparklezVideos
Twitter- bit.ly/CaptainSparklezTweets

Let's Play videos are the biggest things on YouTube right now (outside of music videos), with countless millions of views. What is a Let's Play? Essentially, they're simply recordings of people playing video games and chatting over them, and they're a whole lot of fun to watch. CaptainSparklez is an immensely popular Let's Play creator on the net, and his videos span everything from mod tests to mini-games and even parody music videos done up Minecraft style. Speaking of those music videos, CaptainSparkles currently holds the record for the three most-viewed Minecraft videos period (excluding the official trailer for the game), all of which are music videos. His most popular video "Revenge - A Minecraft Parody of Usher's DJ Got Us Fallin' in Love - Crafted Using Noteblocks" has over 136 million views, making it among the top 300 watched videos ever on YouTube.

Circleight is a master of color and mood, as you can see in this world that is somehow both dark and vibrant at once.

Few players build on the scale that Circleight does, yet her details are also among the game's best. Here we see her Divinus Concientia map.

CIRCLEIGHT

Specialty: Intensely creative and extremely large builds

Can be found at: bit.ly/CircleightMaps

If you ever want to show someone just how amazing Minecraft can be and just how insane the creations can get, Circleight's maps should be your first stop. This girl is a true artist, creating what are arguably the most gorgeous megabuilds of all time. She tends to work with lots and lots of rich colors on massive structures like temples and cathedrals, and she has not had a single map released that was anything short of beautiful. And when we say massive, we mean so dang massive that even on the PC version of the game set to load 16 chunks (which is huge), it's hard to load even one side of a Circleight structure at once. If you feel like checking out her thoroughly inventive and awe-inspiring builds, we'd suggest starting with the awesome Xenohasia building or the very well-done adventure map Desino City.

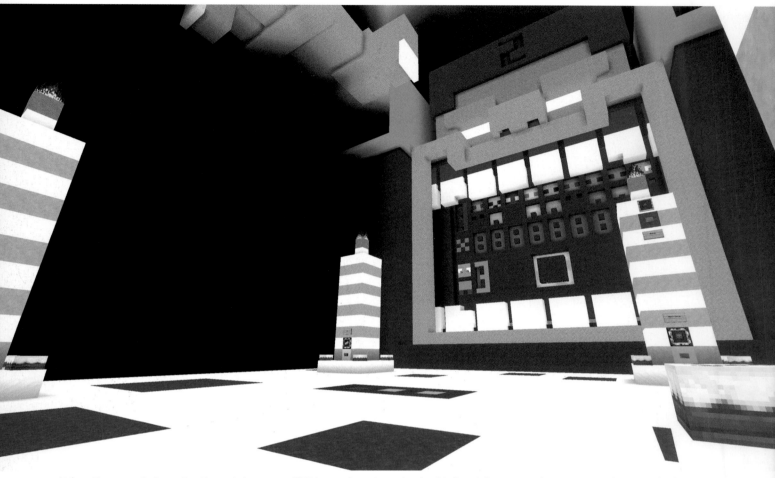

When it comes to imaginative mini-games, FVDisco takes the cake. In this level, however, the point is to keep mobs from taking your cake!

FVDISCO

Specialty: Redstone mad genius, mostly builds mini-games, created the oCd Texture Pack

Can be found at: Homepage- www.ocddisco.com
YouTube- bit.ly/FVDiscoYouTube
Twitter- bit.ly/FVDiscoTwitter
PlanetMinecraft- bit.ly/discoPMC

Being able to build working complex mechanisms with Redstone is impressive enough on its own, but Crafter FVDisco (aka disco_) goes far above and beyond when it comes to Redstone builds. Not only are his builds genius from an engineering standpoint, they're also made to be a heck of a lot of fun, almost always featuring a mini-game of some sort. Even more impressive, FVDisco is so very careful about what blocks are placed where that he has a style of building that is immediately recognizable, something few Crafters ever achieve. Part of disco's unique aesthetic comes from the oCd Texture Pack he created for his own builds, which is one of the cleanest, brightest and most fun texture packs available. Jump over to disco's PlanetMinecraft page and snag a few of his maps if you're looking for a little bit of mini-game fun that'll make you go, "Wow, how did he do this?!"

Nebris jsano19 SethBling Guude kurtmac oldGand Dinner McGamer VintageBe

o> next we ban invisibility!

As leader of the MindCrack group, one of the most prestigious and awesome in the game, Guude sets up sessions like the Ultra Hardcore competition, which can be found on YouTube.

GUUDE/MINDCRACK

Specialty: Let's Play videos on YouTube, creator and leader of the MindCrack server

Can be found at: Homepage- www.mindcracklp.com
YouTube- bit.ly/GuudeYouTube
Twitter- bit.ly/GuudeTweets

MindCrack is a very special part of the Minecraft community. It's a group and a Minecraft server that often put out videos of gameplay on the server or with the group, which itself features many of the most popular Minecraft players in the world. This includes players SethBling, pauseunpause, kurtmac, BdoubleO100, Generikb, Etho, Nebris, Vechs and more, and it is run by the inimitable Guude. Essentially, Guude has created a group and a server where only the best of the best of the Minecraft world can get together and build and play, and they then release recordings of the amazing and hilarious things they get up to on their own YouTube channels. These videos are some of the most-watched on the website, and can feature everything from adventure map Let's Plays to highly competitive competitions, such as the long-running Ultra HardCore (UHC) contest which pits MindCrack members against each other in small groups, with the goal being to have your team survive the longest in a world where only Golden Apples can be used to heal. They're immensely fun to watch and often feature new mods, options and guest stars, such as when UHC 16 included a constantly shrinking world border and Mojang employee and Minecraft game developer Dinnerbone playing on a team.

MINECRAFT, YOUTUBE AND A NEW KIND OF STAR:

An Interview with TheDiamondMinecart
Daniel "TheDiamondMinecart" Middleton • YouTube Creator

YOUTUBE IS THE FUTURE OF ENTERTAINMENT.

More than movies, more than TV, more than music, the world of YouTube channels and the hugely popular personalities that run them is one of the fastest growing entertainment forms in the world, especially with kids. In fact, according to a poll taken by *Variety* magazine, teenagers are now far more likely to recognize YouTube stars than they are the most famous actors in the world (the most-recognized non-YouTuber, Paul Walker, came in at a distant 6th place in the poll).

Here we see TDM in his custom skin along with his popular video characters Dr. Trayaurus and his skeleton dog Grim.

To put it even more into perspective, the videos YouTube stars make on their channels often out-do huge music videos and movie trailers to become the most watched things on YouTube, and the medium racks up many billions of views every month. That's right: billions, and it's not all just for fun either. Through the ads program which shows advertisements before or alongside videos, YouTube channel-runners are able to make actual money from their videos. When those videos start to earn thousands, then millions of views, they earn more money with every view, making YouTube channels not only quite popular, but quite lucrative as well.

Much of what these suddenly super-famous YouTube stars focus on in their videos is that other titan of the "new" entertainment, video gaming. Particularly, stars upload sessions of themselves playing and reacting to their favorite games in a genre of video know as the Let's Play, a phenomenon in its own right that sits within the overall YouTube phenomenon.

Daniel Middleton is one such YouTuber who has combined this idea of Let's Play YouTube videos with the world's most popular video game, Minecraft. His channel is called TheDiamondMinecart **(https:// www.youtube.com/user/TheDiamondMinecart),** and on it he uploads Let's Plays of Minecraft just about every day. TheDiamondMinecart, or TDM as it's known, has a very large following, with 15+ videos with over 5 million views, 200+ with over 1 million, and as of the writing of this book, 3,349,246 subscribers to his channel on YouTube.

That last number is more people than live in the city of Chicago by about 500k. To call it impressive is to understate massively, but how does this all work?

What exactly do YouTubers like Dan do, and how does it get so popular?

We asked Dan to describe the YouTube channel-runner's job, and this is how he put it: "My job consists of using my imagination for cool new video ideas, recording those ideas within Minecraft (and sometimes other games too!), taking those recordings and editing them together to create the final piece and then creating the artwork to go with the video when it goes live on YouTube." Though to the casual viewer it may look similar to regular gaming, Dan says that there's a lot more to it than that, adding "I do get to play and record video games every day, but there's also a lot of behind-the-scenes too."

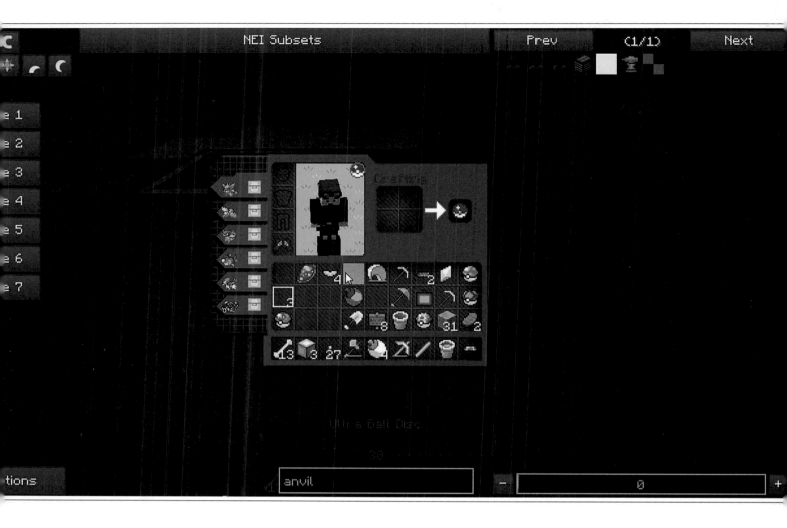

Anyone can start a YouTube channel with just a few clicks, but it takes gaming know-how, special recording equipment (such as high fidelity microphones and powerful video capture software), passion, dedication and not just a little charisma to gain a following like that of Dan and his fellow YouTube stars. As he says, it doesn't happen overnight, but took months of work and practice before he really hit a chord with viewers and his channel took off. "I would say my first big break was over the summer of 2013. I had been making Minecraft videos everyday for a few months, but when the summer hit and I started showcasing Mods for the game and bringing my own stories into those videos, people seemed to really connect with them and it has got me to where I am today."

The 22 year-old says that his channel's growth from a small following to his millions of subscribers happened "Very quick!", adding "I literally just finished my university degree and education as a whole and over the summer, the YouTube channel exploded." But in one way it's no surprise that he'd fit so well into the Let's Play world. Dan is and always has been a passionate gamer, telling us, "I have always been a huge fan of video games, playing since I was very young, all the way up until now. They have always been a big part of my life; I have dabbled in video game design, digital art, animation and simply just playing games while going through education, and the website YouTube gives me the perfect platform to show my video creations to the world."

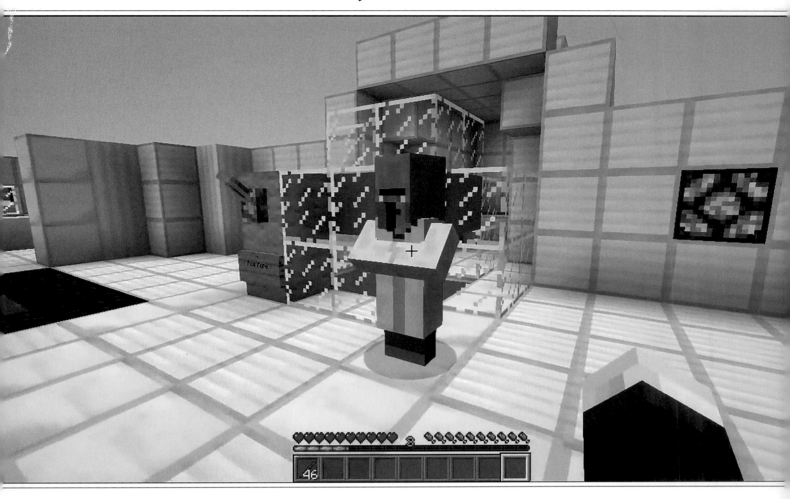

With gaming being bigger than it ever has been, it's the ideal time for game-based YouTubers to make their mark, and Dan believes things are only going to get bigger for video games. "I think the gaming industry is really at a peak right now," he said, "with the internet being so powerful in the creation and growth of video games. You don't have to be a big developer with a huge team any more to create a smash hit game, just an idea and the passion to put it together, just like with Minecraft. I'd say the industry will continue to grow with the importance of the internet and I also think eSports are another huge way of getting gaming out to the masses."

For those who think YouTube Creator sounds like a fun job, Dan has a lot of encouraging advice, telling kids who are looking to start their own channel, "Make sure you're having fun doing what you do. If you aren't having fun making a video, your viewers will be able to tell. So as long as you are having fun doing YouTube then keep at it! Getting popular doesn't happen overnight so be patient, and maybe you'll find one of your great creations go far!"

And don't worry if you don't know what you're doing right away; Dan learned his skills on the job! "The whole process of starting a YouTube channel with

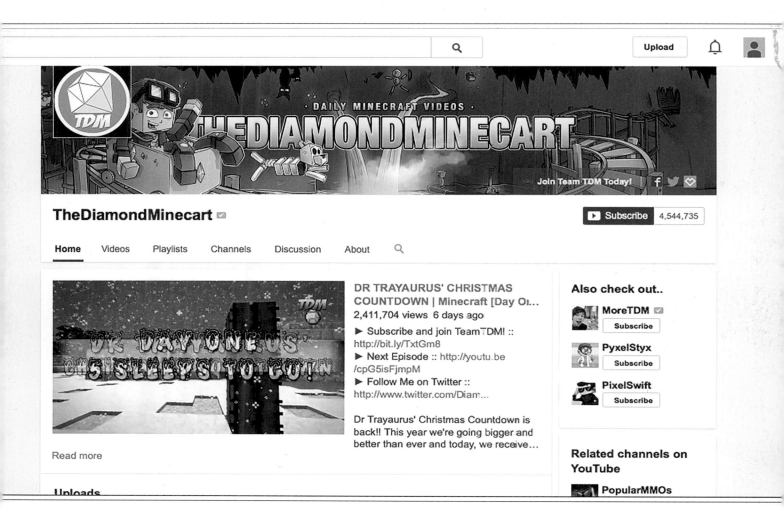

limited knowledge of how it works and the programs/ games you are working with is really fascinating, so starting from knowing everything really wouldn't be the same. The best part of being a YouTuber is that you can create whatever you want, while learning new skills all the time."

Though it only takes one look at a TheDiamondMinecart video to see that Dan is a young man with heaps of both talent and personality, he is nothing but humble and appreciative about his success, telling us, "I am very privileged to be able to have [TheDiamondMinecart] as my full time job."

Whether you're a gamer, have another interest or simply want to talk to the world, YouTube is a place where you can start sharing your thoughts with almost no set up and at no cost, making it one of the most accessible entertainment industries in history. All you need is a free channel, a way to record, a little software, an idea, and some time. And who knows? You might just be the next YouTube star that all the kids are talking about.